. . . to die for

The Gifts of Being Present
Through Loss and Grief

. . . to die for

The Gifts of Being Present
Through Loss and Grief

Anne O'Boyle Vlahos

BEYOND
BELIEF
—PUBLISHING—
YOU HOLD THE FUTURE IN YOUR HANDS

This book is dedicated to my family, both those alive and passed, whose love, guidance, examples, tolerance, and support have aided me in my journey to discover the gifts that are hidden in the loss of loved ones.

Acknowledgments

So much has inspired and supported me as I've written and published this book. I'd like to recognize and thank some of those crucial in helping me deliver my messages.

Firstly, I am grateful for the love, generosity, patience, faith, and gentle guidance of my parents and for the eventual losses of my mom and dad, which provided the intensely personal basis for this book.

I extend my gratitude to Reverend Ella from Villa Marie Clair Hospice, who provided the initial suggestion to write a book about my experiences; she was the first to make me aware that my approach, experience, and process should be shared.

Dean, my husband, is a source of quiet strength and love for me. Not only did he allow me the space to engage fully when my parents were in their time of need, he has such respectful, loving ways. I value his ability to graciously choose silence at times to allow me the space for reflection. His quiet support and deep trust are anchors for us as we evolve. I am also grateful for each single thing he did for our children and me during the process of both these losses: birthday celebrations; bringing our children for visits; ensuring they had proper attire for the services; being a pallbearer for my mom and dad; listening for hours while I cried, sharing what I was going through; supporting me in writing this book, the gifts of a laptop and handcrafted pen to encourage me; and lastly, for the warm hugs that always make me feel loved and safe. I am lucky to have fallen in love so many times with the same man.

Our daughter, Elaina, wise beyond her years, allowed me much of her time to be fully open and share many of these experiences as they happened. Our deep reflections and conversations, short and long, leave me grateful and honored to be her mom.

Karsten, our son, helped me by knowing exactly when to support me or to let me cry or even to joke me out of a funk. It is wonderful to see him be supportive and aware and to understand deeply the meaning of family and responsibility. I am privileged to be his mom.

I'm grateful for my sister Mary—for her deep respect, understanding, and love as we went through the health crises and deaths of our parents. Her perfect balance of support, gentle encouragement, and patience made these losses and coming to closure of their affairs much easier for me. Our closeness growing up and family experiences paved a path so familiar, it rose up for me just when I needed it. I love my big sister.

I really wanted to share this story, but the thought of doing so was leaving me feeling exposed. The support of these dear ones helped me through my concerns and the birth of this book.

The generosity of time and help from extended family, friends, and neighbors as I processed these passings and the aftermath has made these people stars in my sky: Joe, Ginny, Cheryl, Bob, Edie Anne, Jackie, Shaun, Gary, Nina, Kimmi, Veronica, Pat, Don, Chris, Marlene, and many other friends who lent a shoulder when I needed one.

The staff at St. Barnabus Burn Unit and Villa Marie Clair Hospice will always have my gratitude and admiration; they not only marveled us with their expert, compassionate care of our parents, but also with their attentiveness to our family.

There are many spiritual teachers who may or may not know the profound impact they had on my journey, in particular: Shirley MacLaine, Evelyn Isadore, Veronica Sauter, Jarrad Hewett, and Panache Desai. Thank you with love and gratitude for helping me see who I am and teaching me to greet each event and emotion with awareness.

Lastly, I'm thankful for Maura and Keith Leon and all at Beyond Belief Publishing, especially Jess Steinman and Autumn Carlton, who helped me overcome by inertia and spill my heart, love, and hope onto these pages in a cathartic and joyful manner.

A quick note about the title: I was raised in the suburbs of New York City and certainly picked up and retained some of the unique linguistics and phrases from there. *...to die for* is a phrase we sometimes used when describing an amazing meal, pair of shoes, or experience that was awesome or over the top. I chose this phrase as a title because it accurately describes the amazing gifts I received during the loss and grieving of my parents.

Contents

Foreword

My family kept the concept of death from me. I was kept from my grandmother's funeral when I was five and not told about my other grandmother dying for several days when I was sixteen. Several months later, a friend of mine was murdered at point-blank range, and I begged my mother to attend to the funeral. She reluctantly agreed to take me. That funeral transformed my concept of death in a major way.

All my previous experiences were somber, and this was uplifting, rejuvenating, and people were singing! It was incredible. For me, having grown up Jewish, I was blown away to see an open casket. These people were not afraid of death. They were simply celebrating the life of my good friend, Charles. I felt connected to them and to my friend — more than I ever had in Charles' waking life. That was the first moment I felt myself wanting to embrace mortality and connect with all that was alive around me. I had faith.

Twenty-seven years later, my faith is as strong as ever. I am an acupuncturist, herbalist, and yogi who has treated a lot of terminal patients and shared with them some of my deepest connections. I have grown tremendously through these experiences as I have become close to these patients and friends. They have matured me, created a deeper sense of spiritual longing, and assured me that we all must find a deeper sense of peace in our waking life.

This book explores the process of dying and these connections in a way that invites us to think about these matters ahead of time rather than at a time when we are so emotional. There are many difficult aspects of life; there is not a manual on death. So, as I read this wonderful book, I was frequently reminded this may be as close as we come to having a manual on death that helps us prepare physically, financially, mentally, and spiritually for loss.

One of my true pleasures was watching the author grow as the book progressed, not realizing how much I was also benefitting from her experiences of connection. Anne invites us to explore these connections as they unfold through current experiences, memories, and future considerations. She reminds us that from the first moments we hear about someone's passing or their diagnosis of a terminal illness, something shifts inside us. The world often becomes more profound and sentimental, and we gain a new perspective on life that allows us to be present and appreciative in a deeper way.

In this shift, we begin to evolve spiritually at an accelerated rate, opening to new experiences. Our connections are deeper and more enriching as we discover exactly why life unfolds in the way it does. Anne is our guide through these connections, encouraging us to be emotionally vulnerable while spiritually open. She asks us to be informed and prepared, yet accepting of that which we can't change. In many powerful ways, she questions us about our faith and encourages us to strengthen it to help cope with these paradoxical aspects of mortality.

As Anne points out, there is an interconnectedness that inevitably arises in these situations. Synchronicities that we deem accidental or coincidental become significant and important to the outcome. We witness this so much throughout . . . *to die for,* and it compels us to keep reading to find out what the next connection will be or when the next nugget of truth will occur. We are frequently reminded of the power of acceptance and humility — of how connected we feel when we allow ourselves in this foreign space. We are also reminded of the great power of love and all it heals in its path.

Just as we enter the world unaware of what's to come, we leave with the same lack of awareness. However, the experiences we gather as we grow and mature give us a hand up for our exit. These human experiences of love, loss, grief, sadness, anger, and fear all teach us valuable life lessons we cannot learn from a book. Anne realizes this and instead teaches us to use those lessons fully to prepare us for the most inevitable aspects of our lives.

Anne is the voice of so many of us who grew up sheltered from these experiences and who now want to come out of that darkness and allow that love light to shine. Through humor and humility, tears and laughter, anxiety and fear, Anne speaks directly and practically about a topic all of us must face, and provides us with an amazing framework to be successful.

Akhil Kumar Kaplan, MSOM, LAc, Dipl OM

Nationally Board-Certified Acupuncturist and Herbalist

Founder of Three Moons Wellness Center in Waitsfield, Vermont

Introduction

This book, although about death, is really about hope. It's about being open to allowing gifts to come into your life during some of the most challenging times. I began to question my understandings and beliefs around death when I was twenty. It's taken me over thirty years to have that crystallize for me. This book shares my journey, story, thoughts, and experiences, to offer some new thoughts or patterns for you to consider and help you look at death in a way that is actually positive.

As you read this book, I encourage you to laugh along with me, cry along with me, question me, and to explore things outside of this book in order to make it of highest value to you. As I wrote this, there were moments when I laughed, cried, and struggled to find the words to clearly depict my experiences. Perhaps these words will stimulate your thoughts and questions, and allow your beliefs to evolve so that you too can see gifts arise from death.

I found myself spontaneously in conversations with others, speaking about the loss of a loved one; this happened with friends and coworkers, even accidentally with people I would talk to along my travels. I discovered familiar themes that were coming up along the way; this gave me confidence that the story I am telling is one that resonates with people, one that is true. It made space for the idea that there can actually be positives along with the negatives. . . . *to die for* has helped me sort and witness my thoughts and how I've evolved. The result has alleviated many of my fears about the future, helped me live more rooted in the present, and revel in the love that abounds in my life on a daily basis. It's with gratitude that I welcome you to read this book and explore with me what gifts you, too, may find in loss.

CHAPTER ONE

_____

The News—
The Shock of Finding Out

THERE'S NO WAY OF CONTROLLING WHEN AND HOW THE MESSAGE COMES TO YOU

Life happens. As much as we would like to think that we have plans, a timetable, or expectations, life just happens. When we consider something like death, it is simply another event in the course of our lives. It may be an event that is important in your life, but it is one that is an unavoidable event, many times over, in the process of life. It approaches, then appears, like an appointment, an accidental meeting of a friend, a rainstorm. Most times, our first challenge is to come to grips with how little control we have when this information comes to us. What we do have control over is how we respond to it.

I Didn't Expect This: The News About My Mom

So, I'm a little bit different in that I recognize that I have a gift of clairaudience. *Clairaudience* is the power or faculty of hearing something not present to the ear but regarded as having objective reality (according to Merriam-Webster's *Collegiate Dictionary*). Sometimes I hear things that are not said out loud; sometimes it's simply something that I hear, and sometimes it's said by the voice of someone I know who is no longer alive. In the case of learning about my mother's life coming to an end, I actually got that news from my uncle, my mom's only brother, Joe.

It happened one evening when I was driving for work, from New Jersey to Maryland. Near the Reading/ York, Pennsylvania, area, I seemed to get caught up and couldn't easily find my way. I realized that it was an area where a lot of my relatives lived. It dawned on me that I should shut the music off and take a moment to be still, be quiet. I should probably mention here that my uncle had already passed on several years earlier.

Once I parked and became still, as clear as if he were sitting in the car with me, I heard my uncle's voice saying, "Anne, I just want you to know that I'm going to be coming for your mother very soon. I wanted to let you know that it's okay, and I'm going to be here for her. I don't want you to worry, and I don't want you to get anxious."

In response to that, I said, "Wow, okay. Thank you very much for letting me know."

I was always very close to him, and I fiercely trusted him. Ironically, after that information came to me, I actually felt a bit energized. I knew I needed to tell someone else about this, perhaps to keep a record of it.

As a result, I immediately called my friend Jackie and said, "Hey, I have something to share with you. I'm telling you this because I want to make sure that I share this, and you can remind me of it when this event happens."

We had a very open relationship in which sharing these types of things was natural.

In response, she said, "Wow, how do you feel about that?"

I answered, "Well, I am kind of glad that I know that it's coming. I trust that I was supposed to know ahead of time."

As things moved forward, I went back to my regular, busy life—working wife and mom—and a week or so later, I was traveling through New Jersey, where my parents lived, with my children for a winter's break vacation. We stayed with my parents one night, went off to Baltimore for a few days, came back through New Jersey, and stayed with my parents one more night before returning to Vermont. When we were leaving from my parents' home in New Jersey the next day to return home to Vermont, we packed up the car, had our goodbye hugs and kisses, and got in the car to leave. As I looked up from my seat at the wheel and saw my mom and dad standing on the back porch of their home, I briefly remembered what my uncle had said to me, and I made it a point to get out of the car, go back up the stairs, and hug my mom one more time, and tell her that I loved her. I just did it.

At the time, I justified it by telling myself: *You never know. This may be the last time I get a chance to really hug her.*

I was comforted to do it in that moment.

About a week and a half later, I was preparing to make one of my mom's recipes for dinner for my family at home in Vermont. I didn't feel like bothering to look up the recipe that my mom had typed for me, rather, I figured: *Let me call Mom and ask her.*

When I called the house, my father answered the phone and I could hear him, but he was fumbling and dropping the phone, which I thought was him being a little bit clumsy. When he finally settled the phone in his hands, he said, "Oh, Anne, you heard already?"

I responded, "Heard what? What are you talking about?"

He replied, "Your mother had a little accident."

Getting alarmed, I said, "Tell me about it. What happened?"

He then told me the story that was the beginning of her end.

"Well, she was cooking lunch for us, and when she reached over the stove to grab the teapot, her sleeve caught on fire, and it went across her back and down her other arm. I was in the back room, and I didn't know it was happening. When I heard her call out, I ran to her right away. By the time I came out, she was on fire. I was putting it out with my hands. I called 911 and the police came quickly first and then an ambulance right after. They took us both to the hospital, but then your mother got moved to the burn unit at a different hospital, and she's there now."

That's the story, or perhaps a two-part story, of how I found out about my mom. I assured my dad that I would leave in ten minutes to join him, which was about a six-hour drive away, and hung up. Next, I turned to my husband, and shared The News with him. *The News* is capitalized throughout the book to signify the information about health or life status of a loved one that can be traumatizing.

As we had a few different beliefs and did not speak much about spirituality or my clairaudience, I explained, "I want to let you know that my uncle told me about three weeks ago that he was coming for my mother, and I just found out that she's had a bad accident, and she's in the hospital. I know what this is; I'm packing my bag and I'm leaving, and I'm not quite sure when I'm going to come back."

He looked at me and he said, "Oh my God! Do what you have to do. I'll take care of everything here for us."

When I was driving to New Jersey, I called the hospital where my mother was, and the nurse who responded asked me to pull over and said she wanted me to understand that what had happened was very serious. Although Mom had been burned *only* on 21 or 23 percent of her body, it was a very serious burn for a person her age, eighty-four. That nurse also would guide me to go to my dad's first, and then come to the hospital the next morning. I arrived at my parent's home around midnight.

The next morning, my dad and I saw my mom at the hospital.

When we walked in, she said, "Oh my God, I'm glad you're here!"

I responded, "Us too! Are you doing okay?"

"I was so frightened earlier today! I thought I was dying."

Gulp.

I reassured, "Okay, Mom. Well, we're here with you now, and we'll do whatever we can to help you. Let's talk to the doctors and find out what's going on."

Thinking back to that talk with my uncle, it now had an even more profound meaning. The way in which my mom was burned left her face looking fine; her hair was untouched. And although everything sort of looked fine, I couldn't hug her because she was burned on the back of her arms and across her back. There was no way for me to hug her again, ever.

When I go back to that story with my uncle, I think: *Wow, what a gift,* because I had a last chance to consciously enjoy that last hug with her, feel her loving warmth in my arms, and to recall the smell of her in my mind. It was beautiful! So, I was grateful. Very, very grateful.

The morning after my mother had her accident, my dad and I met with her two burn surgeon specialists, and they made us aware of the extent of her injuries. It was a steep learning curve for us. The most shocking thing they conveyed was that they had never had a person her age and with this extent of injuries survive. They wanted us to know the severity of it, and as a result, we had a choice to make.

The choice was, "Do you want to make her comfortable while she passes away in a few days, or do you want to take a chance and go through some very difficult grafting surgeries?"

They had a very, very non-optimistic view of what might happen as a result of surgery.

The shock of this was tremendous to my dad and me. The unvarnished truth of what they conveyed was that she would die then, or she'd likely die later.

No matter what they did, she was more likely to die from these burns than survive. Her chances of survival were very slim.

"What do you want to do?" It was that inevitable.

"Do we want to try?"

The last thing we wanted to do in the face of this reality was to just give up right at the start. We relied on what we knew about my mom, how much of a fighter she was, how strong in character she was, how much she had overcome. Would she want to just give up, or would she want to try?

After speaking with my sister, we made the choice to pursue graftings, though we presented this to my mom as the only option. Eventually, after the three surgeries, an infection set in. The infection was not responsive to antibiotics and was causing organ failure. We had to make the decision to let her pass away.

Sometimes You Expect It: The News About My Dad

I didn't expect how it happened with my mother, but I had that three-week notice.

It was like when you know you have a doctor's appointment three months out, then that day comes and you are a little surprised: *Hey, it's now?*

With my dad, it was more that his health had been declining a bit as he aged. I had expected something was going to come up with him.

My mom and dad were very close. Initially, when my mother had passed away, I had thought that maybe my dad wouldn't be with us that much longer, but in fact, that wasn't the case.

The guilt I had in thinking: *Wow, he's still with us!* is another topic.

As it happened, my father was with us for an additional seven years after my mother passed away. He was eighty-nine at the time of his passing. His health had declined. He was getting a bit more frail and slow, but on the other hand, he was still walking quite a bit, about three to five miles a day, every morning. He enjoyed that but mentioned that he was *losing his pep.* He said he wasn't feeling like himself, as good as he had felt.

I took that to heart, and during my next visit to New Jersey, I learned that he was having some issues; there were some typical older-guy prostate issues. He had gone to the doctor and been prescribed some medications. When I came to visit a few weeks later, I noticed that he seemed a little bit more defiant and in a lot of pain, so I insisted on a doctor's appointment while we were there. We went to the doctor, and, during the exam, the doctor had an interesting look on his face, which immediately startled me a bit. He asked us to get an MRI, which we had done later that day.

Before we left his office, the doctor said, "You may not want to leave him alone this weekend."

I said, "Okay, but I do have to go for a quick trip to Vermont. I'll make it back soon."

He said, "We'll see."

I had to go home because there were a few things that I had to take care of with my family. I drove home on

Saturday and planned to come back either Sunday or Monday.

When I was only about an hour from home that Saturday, the doctor called my cell phone and said, "You're going to want to pull over. I will wait while you do."

A feeling of dread flooded my body. I was on a highway, but I immediately pulled over and stopped. He told me that he did see something concerning in my father's MRI. My dad had stage IV prostate cancer, and it had metastasized outside the area and into his bones.

Here was a guy who, even at that point, had been walking every morning. He enjoyed putting the neighbors' newspapers in between their outer screen doors and inner house doors, or moving their trash out to the curb for them. He very much enjoyed helping his neighbors. He was an original great neighbor. I had not known that his walks had grown quite short in the past month, but still, it was hard to comprehend how a guy could do all that and then jump to stage IV unexpectedly or quickly.

This was quite hard for me; there's a part of you that recognizes stage IV is pretty much the end of the road and then another part of you that is in denial and feeling like: *How are we here this quickly?*

What I later came to appreciate is that the two months of time that we were allowed — like the five weeks with my mother — was actually a gift.

Sometimes It Just Happens

Whether you are expecting it or not, this type of information comes with a tremendous sense of finality, and you can resist it, but no matter what you do or think, it does not change the reality of what you've been told. It's almost like the weather; you can wish that it wasn't raining, you can wish that it wasn't snowing, or you can really enjoy a sunny day, but those are all weather events that you don't have control over.

Surrendering to the message that's being delivered is a first and important step. You can move to the past and wish it didn't happen, or you can jump ahead to the future, when you envision losing them. Or, maybe it's sudden and you've lost them. Remaining present with that news and with exactly what is happening at that moment is so important. Staying present can be quite a challenge; however, breathing — simply remembering to breathe — helps tremendously.

If you can coach yourself or others to take a deep breath every time you get caught up in going forward or backward, you reconnect, almost involuntarily, with your body and the present time. Something as simple as consciously hearing your breath, feeling your lungs fill up, and listening to the air exhale from your lungs brings you fully back to your body and the present moment. In times of extreme stress, I also place my hand over my heart. The sound of my breath and the beating of my heart are comforting and centering.

It is important to do this, to take a moment and be grounded in the present. For in the present, there are many gifts that emerge. I have found that drawing myself present during those times, between hearing The News and their passing, allowed me to witness, feel, and process so much more. As odd as it sounds, the five weeks with my mother and the two months with my father were times I was and still am grateful for, as they were filled with events that proved to contain profound learnings and blessings for me. To be clear, these times were not devoid of pain, anxiety, or fear; even now, I am not sure I fully remember how I got through either one of these events, but what I know for sure is that I am still counting the gifts I received along with the pain.

THE NEWS: PARALYZING, A CALL TO ACTION, OR A MIXTURE OF BOTH

When you learn that a loved one is in a crisis that will likely result in the end of their life, you may panic, you may be in denial, or you may want to try to fix everything. In those moments, it is also good to push yourself to grasp the difference between what you may want versus what experience your loved one may want.

This came to me in many ways:

- Do they want to fight or accept the illness?

- How do you greet that person when you go into their hospital or hospice room?

- How do you manage or interact with the people who take care of your loved one?

- How do you manage the discussions with other family members and loved ones?

So much comes up that it is important to remember to ground yourself because each step is a choice. Each step is a choice to come to terms with things, to be present, to be reactive, to be responsive; your choices can have significant impact on both your experience and that of your loved one.

Protecting Ourselves From Loss: Acting, Not Thinking

When I see conflict or issues, it is my nature to jump in. It is not because I enjoy conflict, and it is not because I love problems. I love to see them resolved. When I was dealing with these crises with my parents, I learned that this natural tendency of mine was not necessarily always the best thing. I recall times with my dad when he was in a rehabilitation center; these were some of my truly heartbreaking stories.

I had mentioned previously that between the visit with my dad to the doctor and for the MRI, I traveled back home on a Saturday for a few days. We had agreed I would come back in time to take him to an ophthalmologist appointment on Tuesday. I was now worried about the information about his health that I had, but he did not. When I was returning to his home on Monday, I called him and learned that he had fallen in the house and was having a hard time with pain. Since I was en route, I had to call the doctor's office and have them call 911 to have him brought to the hospital.

Three hours later, I arrived at the New Jersey hospital where he had been taken. I was anxious, yet relieved, knowing he had been in so much pain but it was now being addressed. I was worried for him. When I walked into the ER, I saw him sitting in a wheelchair in the general waiting room and that broke my heart. In my mind's eye, I thought that he had already been settled comfortably into a room, waiting in a bed or on a stretcher, and out of the chilly reception area with someone attending to him. As a matter of fact, he looked like a sad, lonely old man by himself in the ER, and it tore me up.

Right away, I wanted to go to the desk and scream. I wanted to fire questions off, "Where is he in the queue? Where is his doctor? What are we doing here? He's in tremendous pain! He's freezing cold! Didn't someone give him a blanket?! How can someone be dropped off by ambulance and left in the reception area?"

I immediately started my pattern of problem-reaction-solution, instead of slowing it down, breathing, taking it in, and spending some moments with him first.

Also, what I was doing was unlike my dad's old-fashioned manner: *Wait your turn. Everything in its due time.*

Though I had not raised my voice or fast-fired questions at the admitting desk, some of the things that I was doing actually made him uncomfortable.

I experienced several other incidents at the hospital. I was offered ample additional opportunities to refine my approach at a rehabilitation center where he was transferred for several weeks. As I lived about six hours away and worked full time, I made great effort to visit every week but could not be there on a daily basis. It was my habit to try and call him several times a day when I was not in town. I say *try* because often he would not pick up the phone when I called.

If I missed him three times in a row, I would call the nursing station to ask for help connecting. During one visit earlier in his stay there, I learned a bit more about why it had been difficult to connect. On this particular visit, I came into his room and became really upset; they had him sitting in a wheelchair on one side of the bed, yet the phone was on the complete other side of the bed where he absolutely could not even try to reach it. As a result, when I called, I couldn't get in touch with him as often. Additionally, I had a brought a plant for his room; it was sitting on the window sill in plain sight, yet no one had watered it and it was dying. These were two of many things I saw that were wrong with the room and his care, and really, the biggest thing that was wrong was that my dad was dying.

The key learning I gained from these experiences was that I didn't realize the kind of ambience I was creating when I walked into that room. My fear, anxiety, and high standards were speaking louder than my love for my father.

My suggested alternative to these kinds of behavior is this: when you are visiting someone in a medical facility, do not focus on everything that is happening around them, but focus first and foremost on your loved one. Joyfully greet them, sit down, share with them, and be present with them. All those other things that haven't been tended to can all be addressed separately.

The person who is a patient in the hospital or hospice is likely confined to that bed, or they're stuck in that wheelchair, or they're stuck in that situation, and you have no idea how they feel about it.

Imagine if they are feeling bad about it and you go in there saying, *Oh my God! The nurse hasn't done this, or, Oh my God! Housekeeping hasn't done this, or, Oh my God, the doctor hasn't been here!*

Perhaps this might make them feel even less empowered and probably worse. Remind yourself that there are choices you can make in how you address these situations that can make them better and accomplish your goals. The most important thing is a conscious connection with that person in the hospital bed.

I had shared this story with a coworker of mine, whose mom was in long-term care for quite a while, and was now faced with a stage IV cancer diagnosis.

I asked him, pointedly, "What do you do when you walk in the room?"

He shared observations and actions similar to mine. I offered my hindsight learnings, "Now that you found out this news in particular, none of that shit matters anymore. What matters is that you're there for her, and you're conscious, aware, and present, lovingly, for her in her passing process. So, next time when you go, maybe keep this in mind."

He shared a beautiful story with me a short time later. He went into his mother's room and, rather than getting caught up in what wasn't right, he listened to her and saw that it was late in the day and she was tired. Instead, he chose to kneel by the side of her bed and hold her hand, rub her arm, and watch her fall asleep. After she fell asleep, he took care of the other things that needed to be addressed. He thanked me for sharing that, though I felt honored to have made a small suggestion that helped. It was another time that I thought that I should really write this book; there were small yet significant things to share.

My mother's health crisis was caused by an accident, and I initially spent way too much energy replaying the past to try to achieve a different outcome, which, of course, was futile. I was so upset that she was in this situation – and could lose her life as a result – that I immediately started thinking that if only my dad had heard her screaming from the kitchen sooner, she might not have been burned as badly. I was a bit angry at my dad, who had proudly refused to get a hearing aid for years, and I thought that maybe, if he had a hearing aid, this would not have happened to my mom. That was a really slippery slope. I mentioned how I was feeling about this to my sister.

Graciously, she righted me straight away, and said, "Whoa! This happened. This is no one's fault. It just happened and it's terrible. The issue is, Mom is really ill and she has burns."

She was unhesitating and straightforward, and it was exactly what I needed to hear to pull me into the present.

I was able to have this reinforced in a group counseling session for patients and significant others held at the same hospital where she was being treated. The facility had an advanced burn unit and had treated victims from 9/11. I joined in with a support group once or twice and found it very helpful for me. It became clear how powerful my will to have my mother healed was, and how it really wasn't about my dad's impaired hearing or my mom being careless. It was an accident; it was no one's fault. So, it became all about how to move forward. Again, I learned that I wasn't being present in the moment and was not respecting whatever process her soul — or his soul — had chosen to take on their way to being birthed into the next world.

Death Brings to Light Unresolved Feelings and Beliefs

There were no visitors other than Dad, my sister, and me during my mom's stay in the burn unit due to the gravity of her condition. Prior to her passing, she hadn't been to see her relatives for quite a long time because they were over three hours away by car. However, both of my parents were very close to their families and kept in touch often on the phone, even though the drive was difficult for them.

Because there had been this physical distance from her family, we decided to do an open casket at her wake to allow a deeper level of closure for our family. Both sides of our family were used to open-casket wakes, and as I was growing up, death was not hidden from me. If someone was ill, if someone had passed away, from the time that I was little, I was always told about it. I was always brought along to wakes and funerals. I would say that I can manage these circumstances without extreme discomfort as a result. Though raised together and in the same manner, my sister and I meet that life event quite differently, even though we were only a year and a half apart. I am unsure why.

My daughter had been exposed to death only once, when my husband's father had passed away, but she was quite young and did not know him well. As we moved to my mother's wake and funeral, I had not put enough consideration into how our children would manage and was thinking more about the extended family, who were much more seasoned when it came to these things.

My daughter was shocked when she walked in and saw my mom; she sat down with my sister's twins. They sat and cried together for quite a while, incorporating this reality. My mother's oldest sister, Annie, sat with them and tried to console them. My son, who was six and a half at the time, was also completely shocked, but it turned into anger for him.

He walked in and then walked right away from the casket, saying, "Who did that to Nana?"

He was very angry. "What happened? Why is she there like that?"

We were lucky to have a funeral director who guided him into another room. Friends and family also had children there, and we moved them into another room. One of my friends brought his dog along, and the dog was wonderful therapy for the children. This quickly brought me an understanding of how death impacts everyone differently. I realized that I could have done much more to prepare our children and that I had been very caught up in myself and my feelings instead.

When my father was in hospice, we didn't have people visiting him there either; he was a private guy, and we were fairly sure he would not have wanted visitors. My sister and I were the only ones with him most of the time; my husband and children came once during that two-week period. Other than that, there were only two other visitors, friends from church. Their visit would provide another amazing learning.

I asked my family to come to the hospice to say goodbye to my dad when we were hearing that the end was near. When they did, my husband, our daughter, and son all reacted quite differently. My husband verbally greeted my father and was very warm, but you could tell he really challenged himself. When I hugged him upon his arrival, he felt understandably tense. Our daughter, who was about to turn nineteen, was angry. She couldn't believe that he was like this. Our son, who was almost fourteen at the time, opened his heart, and tears streamed down his face.

I had already gotten comfortable with this idea of hospice and wasn't sure quite what to expect, yet I found myself faced with three entirely different emotions from the three people I love the most. They were hurting so, and it was a very raw moment. I tried to understand what they needed and what I could do or give each one.

Our daughter had just completed her first year of college and was studying nursing. In her second year, the year after my father's death, she had begun clinical rotations. Ironically, on her first day in clinical, an older gentleman died right in front of her.

As she developed a deeper understanding of the whole process, she came back to me and said, "I wish I had been through that training before I had gone to see

Pop. I would have had a completely different approach to this, and I have respect for what people are doing in hospice. I understand it much more now."

This story offered me the gift of perspective; I learned how much time can change your impressions and approach.

There's No *Right* Way to Handle This

When we first had my father moved into hospice, they had told me that the situation was grave, and that he would pass very quickly. It could be as quick as a day, perhaps three or four days. In response to this, I called my sister and she flew out right away and was there for a few days. It was clear to me that it was uncomfortable for her being there, witnessing this, and being present for it, so much so, that it actually caused some pretty strong physical symptoms in her. We discussed it and agreed it was okay for her to leave; I would be there and was okay to handle it.

It felt like a perfect understanding to me; as accepting as I was about her feelings, she also accepted that I could be there, though I don't think we really understood the *why* for the other. While I tried to reach for reasons why this was difficult for her, she was reaching, at the same time, for an understanding of why this appeared to be easy for me.

As close as you are with someone, it is okay not to know all the answers but simply accept. It is such a fluid situation, and there are many emotions. You are accountable for yourself and for being present for your loved one, in whatever shape that might take. My belief is that this kind of stuff is almost predetermined. The more that you breathe and relax into it, the more you get what you can or what you *should* out of that situation—whether it's tears, anger, frustration, resolution, or acceptance. It's all part of your process.

Plans or hopes for how things should go may also get dashed along the way; we experienced that and found we needed to improvise. When our dad was in the hospital and the medical team started treatment for his prostate cancer, my sister and I had originally thought that the treatment might arrest the cancer and provide pain relief. We had thought that he would be able to come home and actually have some good, quality time at home to enjoy and then enter into a home hospice experience for his passing. We thought it would be nice to freshen up the house and have new carpeting installed throughout and new flooring put into the kitchen of his house to prepare for his final return.

The re-carpeting and new flooring project began while he was at the end of his two-week hospital stay. He was to transfer to a rehabilitation center for approximately one month. I look back and now see that this project was our *hope action.* Life had other plans. A day prior to his transfer to a rehabilitation center, he fell in the hospital, and it was quite a setback, due to the pain he experienced. His pain was never under complete control from that point until he entered hospice.

We knew he wanted to return home and believed that he wanted to die at home, but now, because of our hope action, we had inadvertently closed off the option of bringing him home for hospice or rehabilitation. The house was basically under construction at the time. This is a good example of how we were trying to do something nice, hoping for the highest outcome, and not understanding that, in fact, we had no control over the outcome. As a matter of fact, our actions limited our options at the end of his life. I believe now that this actually guided us to the best solution for our family, though I was filled with angst over it in that earlier moment.

CONVEYING THE NEWS

Every family approaches crisis in a different way. There are many customary and cultural implications. There are also considerations with respect to age and physical or emotional closeness. Though The News must be shared, there is a lot to take into consideration when you are sharing traumatizing information with people who love your loved one very much — probably as much as you, but in a different way. There are no right or wrong ways to do this, but taking that breath, thinking a little bit about how you will do this, versus going at it with fear or panic, can be helpful to you and them. Your decisions here can also make this whole process easier on you.

Recognizing, Accepting, and Using External Communicators

I am not sure if this happens in every family, but it did in ours, with The News for both my mother and father. I quickly figured out who were the key persons I would to speak to in our family about my mother or father. The reason for this was efficiency. Taking or making a lot of phone calls is time consuming; it can also be very draining, talking about the same situations over and over again. Some talking is helpful, because it helps you release some emotions and process, but revisiting the same thing repeatedly leaves you feeling a bit stuck in the past versus being present. It also takes away from whatever else you might have to deal with, such as medical issues and taking care of yourself or your family. I also found the same tactic was applicable at my job and chose only one or two people to communicate with. I also chose what level I would communicate. All details, all the time, are not necessary.

It also became clear to me that I had to articulate my expectations to the people I chose as my key communicators: what information they needed to pass on to others in a timely manner, that they should feel free to share whatever I shared with them, or to respect any guardrails I set on what should not be shared. Sometimes you have a closer relationship with some people and you want to share more, but you don't want all of that shared freely in your workplace. Perhaps, you don't want everything shared with all the family members because of age, or fear, and so on. All details do not need to be communicated to everyone.

I continued to struggle with this when considering what I should share while writing this book. It was my goal to crisply convey certain situations, yet not dishonor or disrespect my parents or anyone in my family by doing so. I believe my heart continues to guide me through this.

The Wishes of the Dying and the Needs of the Living: How to (and How *Not* to) Play God

My parents were in their eighties when they passed away. Theirs was a different generation, one in which the desire to know and understand exactly what was going on medically was not as intense as it was, say, for me, my cousins, second-cousins, or our husbands and our friends of a younger generation. I tried to balance how much information I shared based on with whom I was speaking.

For instance, with my dad's illness, I spoke with one of his brothers I was close to, and also with one of his nieces, Edie. Edie, my cousin, happened to be a nurse, so the level that I could communicate with her was very deep, and she easily understood how to deliver that information to the family. That was an easy communication for me, and I was grateful for her.

I also respected the nature of my parents and that they were very private and modest people. I spent those seven years after my mother had passed away getting to know my father better. I came to an intimate understanding of how he felt about that experience. I also had a compassionate understanding of how much his family welcomed information about his condition and how much they really needed to understand and know about his condition. He was very important to his family. I tried to balance the needs of both.

My dad was also important to his neighbors. My father was one of those guys who taught the new people joining the neighborhood how to be a good neighbor by example. As a result, they cared deeply about him and wanted to know what was going on.

Some of the folks who showed an interest in my dad were people from his parish. My sister and I had gone to Catholic grade school with them and knew the family well. The husband and wife came to visit my dad when he was in rehab and offered him Communion, for which he was very grateful. They came to visit him again when they learned he had moved to hospice. This visit helped trigger a key learning for me and helped reinforce what I had learned about my father's need for privacy. When they came into the room, it was wonderful to see them and to reconnect after more than thirty years. As we talked, I looked over and saw my father becoming agitated.

I comforted him by saying, "Mary and Jack are here, Dad, they wanted to come by and see you, and share their love, prayers, and best wishes for you."

Though well-intended, it was so clear that my father was agitated, that I actually asked them to leave.

There was a part of me that felt sad about that, but I also knew that my dad was a private guy, and he did not want people in there watching him die. My sister and I were pretty much okay, but everybody else, not so much. He was agitated by that visit, the nursing staff noticed and wanted to give him Ativan to help him calm down.

Something inspired me, and I said, "My dad, although he is very spiritual and religious, had also been into yoga, meditation, and all that kind of stuff when I was growing up. Please shut the door and give me some time alone with him. I think I can help him out with this."

They respected my wishes, left, and closed the door.

I walked over, sat on the bed with him, took his hand, and said, "Dad, I know that you're really agitated, but I want to help you. I know that you're upset, because they came to see you, you're dying, and you don't want them to see you like this. What you need to understand is that you meant so much, not only to your family, but to the people in your neighborhood and the people in your community. You weren't a rock star, but you were a kind man who always was helpful, who always was there with a quick laugh and a smile, and who seemed to genuinely enjoy life. As a result, these people care about you, and they want you to know how much you mean to them."

I told him that each time I went back to the house – his house – while he was in the hospital and hospice, neighbors would always come by and ask me how he was doing and want to know what was going on and if they could do something for him or for me.

I tried to help him understand how much those little things that he did made such a big difference in other people's lives. I also knew that he kind of bought into the Catholic way of looking at things, and he was revisiting his life as he lay there dying. He was probably thinking about all the things that he did that weren't as great in his life, and that there were things for which he felt he needed to beg to be forgiven.

I tried to help him understand that if he was going to accept those not-so-great things, he also had to accept all the good things that he did in his life; the little things that he did that meant a lot to those people. When I started talking about that and started to share a couple of stories that the neighbors and the family shared with me, he began to sob and cry. I knew I was getting through to him. He couldn't speak anymore due to the morphine for pain, so his tears signaled to me that he was listening, he heard what I was saying.

I wanted to help him calm down, and decided to guide him through a meditation. We started by focusing on a few deep breaths, relaxing, and bringing a beautiful golden light in through the crown chakra, bringing it down through each of the chakras, one by one, slowly, and then going into the earth and pulling that beautiful green, brown, and blue rich energy back up into the body to ground us in the experience that we were having. I saw his breathing begin to relax, and I saw his face begin to relax, so I knew that he was following me.

I introduced the concept that he should try to understand that he was actually in a really good spot right now and that there was not too much to worry about. I asked him to look at himself, to look down at his body, and to recognize that he was an absolutely beautiful being of light. Then, I asked him to turn around and look at all the energy and the spirits and angels that were there supporting him. I then asked him to look at me and to recognize that I was a being of light as well – that I looked the same, but had a different feel to me – and to look around and behind me, and see all the people who cared, who were there supporting me through this process, and that I, too, was okay.

I continued, "Your body is like a car that you banged up in an accident. You have a car accident, you get out of the car, and then you have an opportunity to find a new car, get into a new one. Your body right now is banged up. But you're still you, and you're all the essence of you. So, endorse those things that you're ashamed of or you don't feel good about. But also, in that process, you have to endorse and own the goodness that you brought in this life too."

This meditation brought incredible peace to him, and to me, through his processing.

The nurses knocked and came back in, and they asked, "What did you do?" in response to his new calmness.

I explained the meditation. Throughout this whole process of my dad's hospice, I decided to fully embrace it. The staff told me that not all embrace the process, but that I wasn't only embracing it, I was actually breaking new ground. I valued the feedback, because I wanted to do what I could to help my father in his passing.

The staff at the hospice were special, spectacular caregivers. In addition to them and family members, I also had friends, for whom I'm grateful. These friendships flexed with my needs at these times and were based more than ever on honest and open sharing. As these things happened — some more spiritual or ethereal than I felt comfortable sharing with my family — I knew people I could turn to and share these experiences. During my dad's illness, I had at least three friends who could take the full impact of my words and emotions and allow me that outlet, so that I could be as fully present as possible during this process. I also was in close contact with a friend, Veronica, who offered remote energy, healing, and insights as well. These connections served as a comforting bridge between my reality and emotions.

In your own journey at the end of a loved one's life, allow space for these friends to come forward — those people you can use for support and to whom you can let out your soul. I found these relationships intense during this process, but the intensity was able to recede back into healthy friendships when the acute crisis had passed.

CHAPTER TWO

Keeping Your Center

EMOTIONS CAN, AND WILL, KNOCK YOU OFF BALANCE

The News, as I call it, is the first heartbreaking moment in the process of losing a loved one, but there can be many other communications and events along the way that are equally or more disturbing. I would like to share with you a few stories that rocked me, how I dealt with them, and learnings that may help you to deal with The News and events in a way that you are present for your loved one and for yourself. Following are a series of examples where I found myself particularly challenged.

Miles Apart

I have previously shared about the phone call I received from my father's doctor with The News about his stage IV prostate cancer, but there were also strong feelings of guilt when I got that call, too. I believe the doctor had strong suspicions that he didn't directly share with us, that he knew things were fairly serious with my dad. I know I didn't follow through with direct questions either. This role was new to me; I didn't want to hear bad news. I was worried about how my dad would react to bad news.

I knew I was in denial about what might be happening when the doctor told me that I maybe wanted to stick around with Dad for the weekend. I had to take care of a few things with my family and decided it would be alright to leave for two days, so I set my father up as best as I thought I could by cooking meals and making things convenient. My dad liked his independence and didn't like being fussed over, and he overstated his abilities at that point. I chose to believe him and thought it would work until Monday, when I would return. After I left, however, I was not always able to get him on the phone when I called and was wondering what was happening. What made it all worse is that I knew he had stage IV prostate cancer, but he had not yet been told. I felt awful.

I finally did catch him on the phone when I was driving down to be with him that Monday, but as he answered, he was fumbling with the phone. He was honest with me, and let me know that he had fallen and that it was painful enough that he couldn't get back up. I felt incredible guilt that I left, and then felt sad that he was alone and couldn't help himself. My heart sank. I told him I would arrange to have an ambulance come, and I would call him back quickly once that was arranged.

It wasn't about me here, but I was sure having a pity party. I didn't listen to the doctor or my intuition. I couldn't even call 911 because I wasn't close by. I had to drive another three hours before I could be with him. It was a crushing lesson on the impact of denial. And it didn't finish there.

I got to the hospital probably about an hour or two after my father got there, and what I found was sufficiently upsetting that the guilt raked again at my heart. My dad looked like he was in such pain, and he also looked sad. He looked cold; they hadn't bothered to bring his sweater or give him a blanket. He had been brought in on a stretcher but then put in a wheelchair to wait. He had been given nothing for his pain.

My love for him and my guilt immediately led me to try to fix it. There happened to be a woman who had an Irish last name at the desk, and she had a bit of a brogue.

Because my maiden name and my father's name is Irish, I began a quick conversation and thought to play on some similarities, some commonalities, yet moved quickly to say, "I'm still wondering why he's been sitting here waiting so long. He's in tremendous pain."

My father was kind of embarrassed and worried that I was speaking up. This was one of those times of generational conflict, and I was at a loss of how to manage it.

I mentioned previously that my father was very hard of hearing, and that complicated the process. At times, he wasn't responding or not answering questions fully because he hadn't heard them. This led many times to the perception by medical professionals that maybe my father wasn't 100 percent *with it,* when he actually was. When I corrected the issue by asking them to speak louder to him, that too created some issues. A painful example of this was our discussion with his physician when he delivered the results of the MRI.

Certainly, an ER is not a very private place to begin with, but the doctor needed to tell him the results of stage IV prostate cancer at quite a volume. As if it wasn't hard enough to sit there and be with my father hearing this diagnosis delivered to him, it was being delivered with a very loud voice. It created such a feeling of inescapability and panic as the truth was literally ringing in my ears. I didn't want to be anywhere else than with my dad, even though I found it difficult to be present with that truth—to be present with my father and to incorporate what was happening. I am sure I tried to avoid the nude beach of emotions we were on, but there was no covering it up.

Assumptions About Care

My father became well enough to leave the hospital after two weeks of radiation and hormone therapy; it was time for him to move to a rehabilitation center to gain strength in hopes of a return to his home. Upon leaving the hospital, one last radiation treatment was left to finish at the hospital. We were told it was no problem for this to be managed by the rehabilitation center. When the appointment arrived, the rehabilitation center arranged to take him, via ambulance, to and from the hospital for his treatment. I was assured all of this would be seamless, and there would be no problems. Between his transfer from the hospital and the date of this appointment, I had decided to go home for a couple days but returned to meet him at the rehabilitation center after his treatment.

When I arrived at the facility, my father had just come back from the treatment. Immediately, I could see that he was in a lot of pain. My dad consistently did not ask for pain meds; he didn't want to bother anyone. During his stay at the rehabilitation center, I learned that when you are a patient in a rehabilitation facility, they do not give medication for pain unless you ask for it, and furthermore, the medication they give is nominal, like aspirin, acetaminophen, or ibuprofen.

I was incredulous about this; how could they really manage the bone pain that he was having, both from the cancer metastasizing to his bones, as well as the fall he had taken in the hospital just days earlier?

When I reached in to hug him in the wheelchair in which he was seated, I realized that, in addition to the discomfort he was feeling from pain, he was soaked. The incontinence pad he was wearing was so unbelievably soaked that it had soaked his pants as well. I was completely heartbroken and enraged that someone hadn't taken care of this basic need. One of the side effects of the prostate cancer — and, in particular, the radiation treatments — is incontinence. I felt bad for my dad; he was a very proud guy, and I was sure that this was both uncomfortable and embarrassing. It was certainly nowhere near the level of care that I expected for him; this facility had a five-star rating.

There was a specific challenge I felt when my mom and then dad were in the hospital or a rehabilitation facility. This challenge was about the delicate balance I felt in a number of areas — the care I felt they deserved and we were paying for, the respect the staff deserved, our relative need in relation with that of other patients, and the general resource constraints that were clear to see. It seemed to me that this challenge was heightened in the rehabilitation facility because there are fewer resources. The number of patients assigned to a nurse or LNA is much higher in most rehabilitation centers versus a hospital because typically, patients' statuses are less critical. As a result, I felt compelled to speak up in a way that was respectful to the staff in the rehabilitation center, while also strongly demanding they provide the basic care that my dad needed.

As I was not able to be there every day, I was even more conscious of that delicate balance. What would they do, or not do, when I wasn't there to ask?

So, there I was, absolutely, wildly irate, ready to ride my broom low and fast around the place about how they were not managing his care to satisfaction. But then, I also knew that I had to rely on these very same people to care for him when I wasn't there. If I ticked them off, maybe he wasn't going to get the care he should have when I was gone, even more so.

I asked myself: *How do I swallow my emotions and still get him to be taken care of properly?*

How do I handle it best?

What a challenge to balance it all!

Quantity Over Quality

Upon heading to rehabilitation, we had high hopes that Dad would be able to gain strength and independence, such that he would be able to come home and enjoy a few more months, maybe even years—and maybe pass on from something else. This is what we were told might become a possibility as the result of his radiation and hormone treatments that he was receiving from his oncologist. We hoped that would be the case.

The rehabilitation facility I chose had a five-star rating. They were eager to tell you about all the different things they had going on for residents. There were socialization opportunities; meals in-room or in the dining room; access to the outside by wheelchair; music, physical, and work therapy; games; current events. There was an abundance of different things that would be done to help him on his way to get better.

But in reality, many of the activities relied on his acceptance of them or his agreement to participate. I also did not realize that each department or individual is in contact with each resident for only a short time. As a result, there is little time for any care provider to gain a true understanding of who that person is; for instance, if the patient's responses are genuine or if the patient truly understands them.

My father was a classic example of what happens as a result. He was of that generation where they did not want to make a fuss, they did not want to be a bother; he was never going to speak up or advocate for himself.

It was simply not in his nature and, if fact, it might have been viewed as vain or rude.

His nature was compounded by having too many people being minor touchpoints for him. He did not have that depth of engagement or level of coordination that took into account addressing his pain, mental status, or comprehension; he was not engaged. He was also hard of hearing, which complicated things more. I understand that these challenges are also due to staffing ratios and billing complexities. What I did not understand or consider at that time was additional care from a private nurse or nursing aide. This could have been a way to better manage my concerns within the facility constraints.

Drug Reactions

My father had been in rehabilitation for about three weeks. I was fortunate during this time to have a supportive employer and the ability to minimize my workload and travel. There was only one conference that I was asked to attend for two days in New Orleans. I woke up the morning of my departure and tried to call my dad. I could not get through to his room, a common occurrence by this point. I called the nursing unit desk to ask them to check on him.

The nurse said they were "trying to get in touch with me," to let me know that my father had been transferred to the hospital because his oxygen saturation level had dropped very low, and he seemed disoriented.

The News evoked a deep sense of panic and helplessness because I was far away. It would be impossible to get home any quicker than I had planned, as flights were full due to the convention. As if to test me more, my flight was delayed. While waiting at the airport, I called the hospital to check on my father, and the nurse told me that he was highly agitated and seemed to be delusional.

What?!

They were trying to figure out what was going on and asked if I could talk to him. They put my father on the phone with me, and indeed he had become delusional. He was saying that they were trying to do things to him, trying to medicate him; he spoke in a way in which it was clear that he was fearful of what they were trying to do to him. I tried calming him down, but I was unable to make any impact. I reassured him I would be there as soon as I could.

Of course, this conversation took place while I was at the airport, where there is minimal opportunity for privacy and, due to his poor hearing, my dad could barely hear me. The content and volume of this call drove me to tears. *My sweet dad is now having a fearful time near the end of his life.* I was confounded. It was clear to me that something was awry, but what? As I was waiting for my delayed plane, I had to come to terms with this News, somehow manage how I was feeling, and digest the fact that I couldn't help him until I got there. Even now, I feel the need to take a breath writing this.

I got to the hospital at about 1:30 in the morning. When I got there, my father was wide awake and very alert. He was in a room with another person who was wildly disoriented, loud, and combative. There was a nurse sitting in there with the two of them. I was shocked by my dad's appearance. He looked agitated, and when I began to speak with him, it became clear something was really wrong. He was in an almost paranoid state, asking me why he was here and saying they were trying to make robots out of everybody — really crazy talk — and it scared me.

I noticed his hospital gown was down off his left shoulder, and I observed the spot where there was a fentanyl patch for pain management. There was incredible inflammation around where the patch was, and his skin was actually broken and scabbed up. I thought that there might have been a reaction to the fentanyl patch and brought that to the nurse's attention. This may have been overlooked, as it had appeared to them that my father may be senile or having a psychotic episode.

Quickly, they took the fentanyl patch off, but then we had a period of about a day where the medication had to clear his body. Then, I needed to advocate for a pain specialist to help; my father was becoming conscious of his pain and was quite uncomfortable. Not fun to do at about 3:00 a.m. I was extremely exhausted, sad, worried, frustrated, and angry but somehow had to find a way to get help for him.

The day of his readmission and the following day were an extremely challenging time for me, and I was emotionally and physically exhausted. After finally getting a pain specialist to see him the first night, I left for a brief period to rest and returned mid-morning. The fentanyl was clearing his system, and he was beginning to come back to himself but not fully.

I tried to help orient him by showing him pictures of our family on the iPad and talking to him, but he still was insisting that there was some kind of a conspiracy, or something else that was going on, and perhaps I was now part of it. It took almost a full day before all this went away, and he returned to his lucid self. At that point, he ate, took regular pain medication, and settled back into who I knew he really was.

A key learning here for me was about self-care. Sleep can never be overrated while dealing with an ongoing crisis; personal exhaustion only makes the emotions harder to control and the rational mind harder to keep present.

Personal Touch

I received a call from the rehabilitation center the morning after they had transferred my dad back to the hospital. I was asked to come pick up my father's belongings when I had a chance — this on top of dealing with the fentanyl reaction that happened under their care. *Queue up the strength please!* I drove over that afternoon to pick up his things and was directed to wait in the lobby while they got his belongings. When they gave them to me, they had literally taken everything from his room and put it into a trash bag; his dirty clothes were in a trash bag inside that larger trash bag. I immediately thought of the George Carlin routine where he notes that your *stuff* is *shit* to everyone else.

It was all I could do to get to my car and deal with how I was feeling. I was enraged that his things were dumped into a trash bag, as if his things were meaningless and his life was over. He actually had a duffle bag in his closet. His things could have easily been packed into that. It too was in the trash bag. I felt it was an incredibly disrespectful way to handle his things. Putting his stuff in a trash bag and handing that to me in the lobby was crushing and felt incredibly insulting. I could only imagine if this had happened and he had died. I was obviously mad, and I know that anger usually covers sadness.

I was sad at the lack of care that he had gotten there, and the lack of consideration for his things seemed to physically represent all that to me. It was far from what my expectations were for a rehab facility; it was a five-star rated facility, after all, and I was nowhere near prepared for how things were handled or how we were treated.

Though I'm told by family and friends that my experience is not unique, I will say my frame of reference for five stars was Amazon.com. When you see five stars, it means people were delighted with their purchase. People are delighted when they stay at a hotel with five stars. Five stars at this facility, however, equated to something less than my five-star expectations.

I called my sister to talk it over, and she helped me understand that this is the way it is. At that point, I started realizing that there was something that I needed to do to raise awareness and change this for others. Each one of us deserves, at the minimum, respect and proper care always — but especially when it's at the end of life, when each memory is recorded like a birth. I was sad to see him receive what I felt was sub-optimal care and this incident, along with the fentanyl reaction, cut deeply.

Accidents Happen

My dad was finally starting to look and feel better after over two weeks in the hospital as the results of his radiation, hormone treatments, and physical therapy showed. He was willing to let me give him a shave. He was up, using a walker with physical therapy; I believed I was starting to see hope in him. I was excited, because I felt that he was going to be able to be with us for a little bit longer. We selected a facility for rehab, and he was going to be moving shortly.

The night before he was to move to rehab, I awoke to a call from the hospital at 2:30 in the morning. My mind immediately jumped to thinking that it's something wrong and horrible, and indeed it was. My father was taking initiative on a few things and apparently had tried to get out of bed to use his urinal. When he did, he fell quite badly. He had banged his back, his hip, and the back of his head. They had x-rayed a few things and found that nothing was broken; they were giving him some pain meds for comfort.

They informed me of his fall, and then they told me he was resting due to the pain medication they had given him. I was told there was no need for me to come in until the morning because he was sleeping.

So, there you are, it's 2:30 in the morning and you just got incredibly upsetting News. How can you fall back to sleep? You need to take care of yourself, you need the rest.

What do you do?

I retreated to my routine habits, practices that I knew could help relax and calm me. I started with some deep breathing and did a meditation where I brought in light through my chakras to help balance me and then pulled that energy down through the earth to ground me. When I get emotional, I pull everything up into my head; when I do that, I become vigilant and not present for what's happening.

When I am centered and present, I'm able to make better choices, respond better to what is happening, and am better able to help others, as well. That was my goal. After about an hour of that, I either hyperventilated myself to sleep or actually relaxed enough to fall asleep. In the morning, I felt a bit better having rested and went into the hospital to learn more.

My Mom's Hospice Time

After my mom had been through all her grafting surgeries and was healing, she was confronted with an infection settling into her body. It was *Clostridium difficile* (C. diff), which is troubling, hard to get rid of, but common in long-term hospitalizations. After a forty-eight-hour push to try to get the infection to recede with all medications, as well as dialysis, her body wasn't able to respond and decrease the infection. At that point, we were told that it was time for us to let her go, that she was going to be passing away from a side effect of the burns. This was a process that would take approximately three to five days.

There were many things that happened in that short period of time, but truly knowing that her days were numbered, I was anxious about when that moment would come. I also wanted very much to be present with her when it happened.

After staying at the hospital through the night the first day after this news, I recognized the overnight on chairs or couches had taken a toll on my father and my sister. Note that I didn't acknowledge that it had taken a toll on me. When we returned home, it was less than comforting because a major spring storm had caused the power to go off and the basement to flood.

When all we needed was a warm bed and solid rest, this was a challenge. I found myself way too tired and emotionally raw to deal with this in the best way possible. At that point, I realized that we were all in this together, and we would go and return from the hospital together, but we would not stay there overnight again. As an alternative, I gave instructions to the nursing staff to call me on my cell phone if she was showing signs of passing, so that I could be there.

When the time came in the early hours, they were calling our house phone instead of my cell phone. I had been sleeping with my cell phone in a pocket of my pajamas, and was so exhausted that I didn't even hear the house phone ringing. They finally reverted to calling my cell phone; the nurse told me she had been trying to call me for forty minutes, and that my mom was now very close to passing. I quickly rose and woke my father with The News. My father and I both wanted to be there.

My dad and I jumped in the car and began the forty-minute drive, trying to get there as quickly and as safely as we could. When we were about twenty minutes from the facility, I felt something brush over the top of my head and rustle my hair. At that point, I knew that my mother had left her body, and she was gently touching me and saying goodbye. I was very grateful for this contact, no matter how sad it made me. When we got to the burn unit, they met us right away when we walked in and confirmed she had passed. We went into her room and spent time with her. It was a very sad yet quiet time in which I realized how glad I was that her suffering was over. Burns are a far more fierce condition than I had ever imagined.

One of the most amazing and comforting things for me at this time was knowing that this nursing staff was highly conscious of the needs of a person in this state. As she had approached her final moments, the nurses gathered around my mother, held hands, and held her hands and were with her while she passed. In particular, the nurse who had been assigned to her when she was brought in was with her when she passed.

I found great comfort in knowing that she was cared for with incredible love, respect, and honor. That same nurse also gave us a copy of a beautiful poem called, *The Dash*. It perfectly conveyed that a person is much more than the dates on which they were born or died; the essence of their life is captured in the dash. I can only say that the experience of how well my mom's care was managed and the sensitivity with which they cared for us as a family, right through to the end, was the finest example of care I have ever experienced. I am eternally grateful to the entire staff of this burn unit and remain in awe of how well that team performed in every step of the journey.

Relief and Release

I had heard others speak about a feeling of relief when you have been waiting for a loved one to pass and the guilt they then felt for feeling this relief. With the passing of both my mom and my dad, I experienced the feeling of relief, but the feeling of guilt did not follow.

I had also heard people often say, "Well, it's okay, because now they're at peace."

That used to sound a bit topical to me, but I began to understand this in a slightly different way; I think it might be that the person left behind is the one now at peace. I knew I was. For me and perhaps for you, the whole time holding vigil while someone is dying, your sole focus is that event. You are waiting for them to die. Just as when someone is in labor, you're waiting for the birth to happen. Ironically, there were feelings for me that were quite similar in both of their deaths that I had experienced with the births of my children. I felt some of the joy that I had felt when my child was finally born when my mom and dad finally passed away.

There is probably a whole lot more here for me to explore with these feelings and their similarities. I get a sense that it is not only a relief that the person is gone and the suffering done; I think that there is some real joy in knowing that we have labored along with them as they birthed their soul from their earthly body. The result is truly a beautiful thing. Like labor and delivery, it is a bit messy, but the result is the liberation of their soul from a body no longer able to provide life's experiences.

Moving on after a loved one departs is a process and can also be a challenge. In anticipation of what might be the outcome of my mom's accident, my sister had read and then given me the book, *The Year of Magical Thinking*. Joan Didion's story was a painful story of her loss and the challenge of moving on. I can easily relate to that because I saw this happen with my father upon the passing of my mother. Though he did the necessary things, such as call insurance, Social Security, and so on, he did not get rid of any of my mother's things. He never completed that process of releasing her.

Further on, I will detail some of my experiences when going through both of my parents' things after my dad had passed.

MAKING DECISIONS: UNDERSTANDING PRIORITIES AND URGENCY

I found when dealing with medical institutions — such as hospitals and rehabilitation centers — insurance policies and institutional processes are in place which usually necessitate things moving along in a timely, prescribed process. As a result, I found myself pushed to make some decisions quickly, while with others I was able to take a little bit of time. Balancing these medical decisions against our parents' and our own wishes was confusing and challenging at times. After each of them passed, the focus changed to what we were going to do to honor them, which brought up a whole new level of confusing and challenging times. Some of these decisions shared that time pressure, while other decisions were made at a more relaxed pace.

The following stories are examples that helped me learn when things were indeed pressing and when I could push back and take the time I needed to do exactly what I felt was right or make a more informed choice.

Care Options: Decisions That Impact Health, Well-Being, and Comfort of the Dying Person and the Family

There were two opportunities for a crash course in choosing care options and facilities for us. Our first choice was considering the rehabilitation options when managing our dad's care, and the second would eventually be choosing hospice care for him. During his time at the hospital, social services gave me literature on options for care in rehabilitation and hospice. I began to explore this while he was under their care.

I found that rehabilitation and hospice fell into about three key categories:

1. Home-based care
2. Generalized long-term care facilities with rehabilitation and hospice units available
3. Hospice-only facilities

The first option, *home-based care,* provided for many variations of care for both rehabilitation and hospice. These seemed to be an excellent alternative but, once we had begun the carpeting and flooring project at his home, those options were closed off until the project was complete. In speaking with family and friends who have done this, there are some challenges with this, too, but it seems to be a very good option for many people. Being able to have that loved one—especially when they are a bit more conscious—know that they are in the comfort of their own home can be reassuring.

The challenges for us focused on the practical and the emotional. Key caregivers must be chosen, in addition to nursing services; care skills must be learned. On the emotional front, some persons may be uncomfortable staying in a home where someone will or has previously passed on or, perhaps, the person departing may not want to burden their family.

The second option, *long-term care facilities,* could manage both rehabilitation and hospice. I visited several of these long-term care facilities we could have chosen. Although we did choose this type of facility for rehabilitation, we would decide against it for hospice; it didn't seem as calm and peaceful as I hoped to find for a hospice experience. This is perhaps a bit strange to say, but the focus there seemed to be more about living. If residents became injured or ill, an ambulance would be called unless a DNR was in place. There were activities for the residents. The mood was more light-hearted and engaged. It seemed filled by people who were still invested in life. For a hospice choice, where you would prepare for death, it did not seem to fit for us.

We began to further explore rehabilitation options after almost two weeks in the hospital, and it became clear he was getting well enough to move. As we were deciding upon an in-house rehabilitation facility, my site visits focused on alternatives that were provided by the hospital and physician. Additionally, there are private and public facilities. It became apparent afterwards to me that there seemed to be some general assumptions that are made by social workers when they present options and guide you. Two key areas of presumption that I noted were regarding cost and proximity.

There was a presumption that we needed a facility whose cost would be mostly covered by insurance. The other presumption was that the facility should be in the surrounding area. We made our decision based upon the different recommendations that they gave us, not fully understanding that the presumptions closed off potential options. I toured the recommended facilities, not fully understanding that there were also private facilities available, where we would need to contribute to the cost.

In the end, I am not sure if we would have also encountered some of the same care quality issues at the unexplored private facilities. I now understand the relevance of not only knowing what you can and cannot bear financially, but the importance of conveying this information, along with additional environmental or care needs you have, to those who counsel you in this area to ensure this is included in the decision-making process.

On proximity, I realized afterwards that I had assumed that choosing a facility nearby would allow for his doctor to continue as the lead on his care. To me, it was a bonus that the facility was only fifteen minutes from his home, where I would stay when in the area. After he was transferred, I learned that each facility has house doctors who come in weekly and manage the care of the residents; so, the advantage I had assumed of continuity with the physician was invalid.

It became obvious to me at this point that, no matter how diligent I had thought I was being, there was a lot I did not know. I beat myself up quite a bit about this at the time and allowed my anxiety and guilt about my decisions to get to me. I now understand the simple truth that there is a lot to know, even when you're under pressure. The source of the guilt was likely misplaced and was more my realization and disappointment that I couldn't change the ultimate outcome. My optimistic nature sometimes clashed with reality and reason.

Next, we were faced with choosing a hospice option. During my dad's second hospital stay, his medical team determined he had reached the point where medical intervention would no longer improve his condition. His physician informed me of this, and social services counseling began again.

I was told, "It is now time to move your father to hospice."

That was on a Thursday, and they wanted to move him the very next day, Friday. They offered me two resident facilities to consider that met our criteria of being *hospice-only*. Due to his high level of pain and his home being under renovation, we all agreed an in-resident facility was our only choice. The first and highly recommended facility was in the Bronx, which is fifteen miles and forty minutes away from where I was staying. This commute is complicated by New York City traffic on both the George Washington Bridge and the Cross-Bronx Expressway; if you needed to travel during rush hour, the journey could easily take much longer.

The other option was closer and private; the guidance seemed to be pointing away from this option because it was private, and the likelihood of our out-of-pocket expenses could be significant depending upon how long he lived. *Yikes.* Just absorb that a moment. It sure took me a while. If he lives longer, it will cost you more. Very pragmatic, yet very distressing.

I was overwhelmed and insisted that I must be able to visit both facilities before making a decision. This did not sit well with the hospital as the time to complete the paperwork for the move was compressed; the social services group did not work weekends. It was finally agreed that my father would be moved on the following Monday instead of the next day. A side learning here was that nothing happens with these kinds of moves on a weekend because it involves paperwork from a team that only works Monday through Friday. I had not realized that this was part of the pressure I was under to move him; I assume this was in addition to insurance concerns.

I visited the two facilities to ensure all options were fully explored. The facility in the Bronx was lovely. It was a hospital that was dedicated to terminally ill patients, so, in effect, it was a hospice, but with a hospital-like environment. To me, although it was a peaceful, reverent, beautiful, and clean facility, it was too far away and hospital-like for me.

The second facility was absolutely perfect. It was tucked away and set on beautiful grounds. It was formerly a private mansion that was converted, first, into a retreat for nuns, but then into this hospice. It also had rooms in which family members could stay. These family rooms had served as dorm rooms for the nuns during retreats. How amazing that there was actually a place where you could physically stay, separate from your loved one's room, so that you did not have to leave the grounds to shower or rest.

As this was a private facility, there were requirements around insurance coverage. After a covered, forty-eight-hour observation period, insurance coverage was determined. Coverage was assured if continuous oxygen or intravenous pain medication were necessary. If this was not the case, the uncovered cost was approximately $500–$600 per day.

My sister and I discussed this and agreed this was the best place for our father, despite potential financial implications. We wanted him to have the best possible setting as he completed his life. Additionally, the rooms here seemed very home-like and seemed to welcome flexibility in customizing the room and environment. As it turned out, after the forty-eight-hour observation period, the nursing director informed me they had determined our father required continuous intravenous pain medication and that his stay would be fully covered by insurance.

Though I should have been relieved to learn this, we had already crossed the bridge on cost a few days prior. My response to this news might have seemed off to the nurse, but it was because I felt uncomfortable with the discussion. I didn't even know how to capture or express what I was feeling. I felt grateful that the cost was being covered, but there was another part of me that had felt honored to pay for this last need of my father.

There may be a broader variety of choices, but these three categories cover most options. It is key to be engaged in researching and exploring your options with the resources provided and additional ones you can identify to ensure the greatest satisfaction in your selection. In hindsight, I would recommend open discussions with family and friends before the need arises. The information gained will surely be of use.

Burial and Service: Do You Know Their Wishes?

Both with my mother and my father, we had the convenience of knowing they were passing ahead of time. I took the opportunity both times to call the funeral parlor ahead of time, to at least set the stage for it, inform them that this was happening, and ask if there was anything that I needed to do or have ready. At the very least, I was comforted by how they responded to me; I was also given a cell phone number, so that I could call at any time. I was grateful for someone to be incredibly kind to me at a time when I felt fragile inside.

My parents were both in their eighties when they passed away, but they were the kind of folks who were still buying ten-year warranties on appliances. It was a beautiful testament to life, but their final wishes hadn't received that attention; they had never even selected a grave site, though they had a simple will. I learned through discussions with family and friends that some people do actually make their wishes known, and quite specifically so, while some are hesitant to fully discuss it, even when approached. For others, the discussion has never been approached.

In any case, I would encourage an open dialogue about final wishes with family. Lacking any discussion, or one not as thorough, can lead to confusion, concern, and even arguments. This discussion, even at a minimal level, makes it a bit easier for the people who are left behind.

A discussion on final wishes may be a tricky one to approach. Since my close-up experience with it, I have found that certain events can give that opening. Events such as the death of a loved one, family member, or friend, The News of a diagnosis or life-threatening situation, or the death or illness of someone famous can provide a stage to witness and discuss what was, or was not, chosen and the feelings and thoughts about it.

After each of my parents passed, it was an opportunity for me to talk about my wishes with my husband and children and to ask about their thoughts and wishes. And, although I know the entire road map is not there, I do have a certain guidance directly from them what they may want and have conveyed what I might want as well. As a result of the tragic loss of five teenagers from our area from an accident, I had the honor of driving my son and several friends to many of the funerals; these children were fifteen and sixteen years old. This type of discussion came up organically when we were talking about the services we attended. These times provide unique opportunities to learn and to guide.

Take a risk and bring this up with your loved ones if they have not discussed it with you already. The discussion doesn't have to be complete; it just needs to start. It begins to bring clarity to a challenging situation but, in some cases, may even bring some relief or comfort that it has been discussed.

Religious beliefs are another strong influence on final wishes and protocol. I am aware that in the Jewish and Muslim faiths, it is desired that the deceased be buried within twenty-four hours or before the next sunset. For my parents' religion, Catholicism, that was not the case. And, even though there are religious traditions, the choice is still yours and there are many ways in which to personalize the service and burial. There is a tremendous richness in that process of the final honoring of your loved one, and the building up or process leading to that final ceremony. By allowing yourself time, it takes some pressure off and may also allow for better preparation and attendance by family and friends. For our parents, though they had passed away on a Tuesday and Sunday, we held the funerals on a Saturday. This allowed us time to prepare and also allowed many distant family members the opportunity to come to the event on a weekend.

Services, like any other event, can be personalized in meaningful ways. We found the time between death and funerals allowed time to add special touches.

Throughout her stay in the intensive care burn unit, my mother had been well cared for by the staff. I know her death was certainly hard on her family, but I am sure it was not easy for those who had cared for her for five weeks, either. It was such a painful end to such a beautiful woman, and I wanted to try to do something special for both those who had cared for her in the hospital and also for her family and friends who adored her. I decided to purchase perennial flowers, had them wrapped up and delivered to the restaurant where we had the repass dinner. As guests left the dinner, we encouraged them to take one or two of those perennials and then plant them in their garden to remember her. Gardening was one of my mom's favorite things.

Her other love was cooking, so for all those nurses who took care of her, I had a flower as well as an herb planted in colorful ceramic pots. With each pot, I wrote a thank-you note, filled with gratitude for their care and also connecting them to my mother's love of gardening and cooking. These parting gifts were well received and, for me, continued a circle of giving that I know my mother practiced regularly. We had also asked that, in lieu of flowers, donations be given to both facilities that cared for our parents. There is a beautiful cycle of giving, even at the end of life, that continues. I found this helpful to me and, in a way, channeled some of my grief in a positive direction.

Estate Resolution

An estate, by definition, is simply the assets and liabilities left by a person at death. It includes what they owned, owed, personal effects, property, and so on. Though the financial value is what is often the focus, I found the process of dealing with the personal effects and the personal side of the finances the most interesting.

My mother's passing was difficult on my father; being there when she got injured, then losing a partner that he'd been with for almost fifty-five years, was a tremendous blow. He would write about this in letters to my mother, after her passing, on special dates like her birthday, their anniversary, or Christmas. My father did not have a desire, nor wanted us, to go through all my mother's things. As a result, my mom's pajamas were still hanging up in her bedroom, her purse was still hanging on the back of the door where she always left it, her hairbrush on her dresser, her toothbrush still in the holder in the bathroom.

I know, initially, this was a real sense of comfort for me. When I would visit my dad in the months after my mother's passing, I could still bury my face in her pajamas and smell her. It reminded me of hugging her, the smell I would get from her when she hugged me back, and even the gift of that last hug that I had with her, prompted by my uncle's visit. Her things remained untouched and frozen in time for over seven years, except for the occasional perusing of my sister and I and our daughters. As time moved on, it was heartwarming to see my daughter posting a picture of her hairbrush with her hair still in it or my niece posting a picture of her wearing my mother's glasses. My father never told me if he, too, visited her through her things; but I learned, after he passed, that he did.

When my dad first went into the hospital and then rehabilitation, I took the opportunity to do a thorough cleaning of the house because I had believed he would be coming home. I washed all his clothes, I washed the towels and bedclothes, I straightened up, all in preparation for him coming home. After I came to the realization that he was never to come home again, I was sad that I was not to have those touchpoints and little memories like I did with my mom. As time passed, though, I realized that the task of clearing out their home still offered many touchpoints for me, only different.

Right after my dad passed on, my sister and I had an initial burst of, "We've got to clear the house out, we have to move things forward, and we've got to do this and that."

After about two rounds of joint visits to the home to clear things out, we agreed to take our time and not to rush, mainly for me. I was not emotionally ready for all we were encountering; we were dealing with both his and her things. As they had lived at the house over fifty years, it was a tremendous amount of stuff to deal with, both their physical items and the memories of them both contained there.

It took us almost a year and a half before we completely emptied out the house and sold it. This time allowed me to go slowly and sort through both her things and his; my knowledge of my parents gained many dimensions, and the slower process allowed for such a richness of appreciation for who they were and their relationship. Though I was close with both my mom and dad, this closeness deepened with them even after they had *left* me.

I recall the first of my mother's items to go to its new owner — a gold crucifix. My mom and my daughter had a sweet, close relationship. I recall the three of us sitting in my mom's bedroom and my daughter going through mom's jewelry. When she came across the crucifix, she directly asked my mom if she could have it after she died. I was shocked and probably said something like, "Don't say that!"

But my mom said, "No, that's fine! I'd love for Elaina to have it."

Well, when my daughter came to their house prior to the wake and funeral, I pulled it out and put it on her, and she was happy to have something of my mom's. Older folks don't have as difficult a time discussing the distribution of their things; it may even be comforting. It sure was to me—a gift my mother was still able to give my daughter.

This was moving for me, yet there were many more touchpoints that I discovered. I kept looking at things saying: *Oh my God!* There were tears. Tears of loss, gratitude; I felt such love. The process of going through things slowly allowed me a genuine and thorough grieving process, one I am grateful for. The understanding of my sister, my husband, and children was welcomed. This time and these experiences added such a richness to my grieving process that I hadn't expected.

When each of my parents had passed, I had found that the love I felt for each of them was strongly associated with their physical presence. Once they passed on and we buried them, I still had all that love but was missing the physical anchor for it. For a while, the grave site and their things became somewhat of a physical avatar of them for me, physically holding space for that dislocated love.

I noticed with both of their deaths that around the five-month mark, the physical love I had for them somehow relocated itself within me, within my heart, and speaking of them became much easier. The only experience I recall that seems at all similar was being pregnant with our children. When I traveled on business trips while pregnant, it was nice; my daughter or my son was right there with me. I instantly knew they were healthy, safe, and loved. I spoke to them constantly. After they were born and I had to travel, I missed having them physically with me, even though I could speak to them on the phone. This process of physically relocating the love that I had for my parents was similar to this but in a reverse process.

Even with the practical job of resolving my dad's finances, I experienced sweet touchpoints. Upon my mother's death, my father ran into some difficulties when he went through resolving my mother's estate, despite having a will in place. As a result, he worked with a legal firm to manage his estate, so that the process after his passing was as easy as possible. He showed me where the documents were and gave clear directions to me. We were to meet with his lawyer after he passed away and be walked through the whole process. It made the business portion of resolving things a lot easier, but, as I was walking through these steps, there was one thing that struck me.

My dad had a couple Certificates of Deposit (CDs) — actually, quite a few of them — but he didn't keep them all in the same bank. Though I'm not quite sure of his rationale for this, there was a time where it started to drive me crazy because I had to drive to several different banks to sign paperwork, show legal documents, and so on. It was certainly time consuming. While getting back into my car after stopping at the third bank one day, it struck me that I was actually retracing my father's footsteps as he was taking thoughtful steps to take care of not only his estate, but taking care of what he wanted to leave as gifts for my sister and me, from what he and my mother were able to create for us.

My parents had come from very modest backgrounds, and he was proud of what they were able to achieve. So, after a period of viewing it as a task, being able to take each one of these steps — literally following in his footsteps — changed my view.

I began to think: *Oh my God, this is cool! I'm actually following in his footsteps, seeing his handwriting and original signatures, signing the same documents, meeting with some of the very same people that he did!"*

It felt like such a sweet hug from him, such a gift — these physical spots where our paths crossed were the exchange of gifts after his passing. The love was palpable and the gifts meant much more to me. I wondered if this step was reassuring to him when he had taken similar steps after my mom had passed.

There were two circumstances that I recall as being particularly difficult, wearing on me in the estate resolution process. The first was the relentless request, each step of the way, to be asked to present his death certificate and, in some cases, my mother's too. Though I knew my parents were dead, the request repeatedly hit me in the heart, and there was a kind of exposed feeling that arose in me. I felt a bit violated that people who didn't even know them or me could access this very private information. I guess, after you're gone, it becomes factual and public. That challenged me.

The second challenge was reading these death certificates over and over. In reading my dad's it was a bit easier. I was there. It had been real for me. The wording was muted, "died of natural causes." In reading my mom's, I got stuck on the time and cause of death. I wasn't there when she passed, so I had to believe the time that was on the document. The cause of death wording was vivid and harsh, "died of complications from burns."

Compounding my difficulty with this reality was poor customer service at two banks. Most bank personnel were kind; however, there were at least two that tore me up. One seemed to make the process lengthy, calling a manager over, calling a central office several times; I was there for over an hour and they didn't once say, "I'm sorry for your loss."

At another bank, I had to deal with two people, both of whom needed coaching in customer service with respect to this. They treated me like they didn't quite believe me, that perhaps I was stealing from my father. I was sad about it and angry later. I am sure they felt they were protecting their eighty-nine-year-old customer, but it was at his daughter's expense.

There are many things that need to be done when a person passes away. It can easily become overwhelming.

Here are things that may help you not to feel overwhelmed:

- Take a breath.
- Seek sound advice.
- Speak with someone else who has been through this.
- Make and revisit a To-Do list.
- Prioritize what really needs to be done right away and what does not.
- Identify what you can ask others to do for you.

- Allow yourself some space and time to get to those things that do not have to be done right away.

As you go through this list, you may find that an organic sense of timing and awareness of your comfort level will arise. If you feel pressed or something feels forced, check in with yourself. If you are unsure, check in about it with someone you trust. By rushing through each step, it does fulfill a certain need to *do something,* but you may find the rushing can also be a type of distraction for you from the process of grief. There are certainly times when situations call for urgency, and you will need to rise to it. When you *can* take your time, understand it's *okay* to take your time. This estate resolution process gives a sense of closure, and helps you come to terms with your grief along the way.

TAKING CARE OF YOURSELF

I tend to be a busy person. I almost overschedule my time, even while telling myself I'm optimistic about what I can achieve. As a result, I allow the schedule, or tasks, to run me, instead of being present to experience my life.

When you're losing a loved one, it's very easy to jump into and get stuck in your head. When you're in your head, you may find yourself jumping back or forward in time. When we jump back, we tend to visit our memories; when jumping forward, we might feel fear, thinking: *What might happen next?*

Both these actions take your focus away from being present and experiencing what is happening. For me, taking a few deep breaths or closing my eyes with my hand over my heart, conscious of its beating, were the tools that forced me to come back to the present and be in my body. Other times, I released pressure in both healthy and unhealthy ways in order to bring me back and ground myself. Whether healthy or unhealthy, these things tended to be focused on rewarding myself in a way I could receive with my five senses. Ironically, sleep didn't play a big role here.

Being Grounded and Present

Both times, with my mother's and then my father's hospitalizations, I did my best to be there as much as possible. I was lucky to have great employers who were supportive of me, taking the *family first* approach. Their support included a flexible schedule, as well as the backup support needed to cover key roles of mine. Because of this, when I would be there with either my father or my mother, I didn't have to be on my computer or constantly on my phone. I also made sure that we weren't watching TV. The key world events that were happening, from my perspective, were usually happening within the four walls of that room.

I did my best to limit distractions when at the hospital, rehab, or hospice facility. But when I was away from there, I tried to do things that would help me. Sometimes it was as simple as going outside and taking a breath of fresh air or taking a short walk. With my dad's illness, I found this small massage place where these sweet Chinese ladies gave incredibly tough massages. And, as a result, there was no way you couldn't be present with your body when they were working on your body! I was there almost once a week to relieve stress and help me get grounded back into my body.

I also did short visualizations frequently, to try to bring light into me, down through my chakras and reaching down into the earth to try to grab some of the Mother Earth energy; this too brought me present. As a result, when I showed up at work, I felt able to be present and on board. I also spent some time speaking with my family or friends; that too helped me sort through the day. Listening to them speak about their day helped too. I recognized early on I had to engage myself in a number of ways to help keep myself focused and present.

There were also some unhealthy distractions that I had. While my dad was in rehab, a friend of ours was doing all the flooring and the carpeting in the house. After a long day for both of us, he was often kind enough to stick around after work and go out to dinner with me, or sit and drink a glass of Bailey's and Stoli together. I know the overindulgence in either eating or drinking wasn't the healthiest thing for me. At the least, I learned that I am, for sure, a stress eater. The drinking, though less of an issue, offered stress relief, but it probably wasn't the best choice either. It certainly wasn't healthy. Another stress activity that I occasionally engaged in was to smoke clove cigarettes. Again, not so good for my health, but it was a way for me to release some stress.

I wasn't at all perfect during these times, but I also was careful to be forgiving of myself when I was doing things that weren't perfect. I became conscious of them and tried to gently redirect myself. I didn't want to dilute the experience of what was happening, nor did I want to come to terms with what was happening (the deaths of my parents) at my own expense. It took me a little time to understand that this was what I was doing.

The Power of Observation

As I observed what was happening with my mom in the hospital, I realized that because she couldn't speak for herself, the caregivers did their best but also made some assumptions. In my mom's case, I noticed there was an assumption that she was Irish because her name was Magdalene O'Boyle. In fact, her family was Slovak; her parents immigrated from Bratislava. Sometimes offering information about the patient can help the staff make some adjustments in how they deliver care. I did this for my mother by creating a posting for her room entitled, "A Bit About Magdalen Martha Pitel O'Boyle," and it seemed to make a difference immediately in how they spoke to her. I noticed that they now called her by her preferred name, Madge, versus Maggie. They no longer referred to her as their Irish Rose, but simply as their beautiful rose. I hoped this meant as much to her as it did to me.

Communicating well and openly and asking honest but not accusatory questions was a good way to develop a great rapport with the hospital and social services staff. In particular, if you can't be there frequently, having a healthy rapport helps both the staff and the family. Many times, you feel helpless when you're there. Asking what you can do to help can also ease your stress and that of your loved one, as long as you are not interfering with care. It could be as simple and active as taking some lotion and massaging their hands or feet or knowing when you should leave the room for a bit. Take that initiative and openly talk, as well. There's a lot to be gained by observing and asking questions, but seek to understand. Care staff is usually very busy but willing to help make the best of things.

Opening Your Heart and Mind to Alternatives

As I went through these two crises, I had at least two really good friends, in addition to my husband and family, to open up to. However, I found it difficult to take the time to *do something*—something like take a friend up on their invitation to lunch, to do something as a family, or go see a movie. The difficulty laid in my fears; I felt that if I stepped away for a minute, if I withdrew my energy at all, it would all go to hell in a handbasket.

Most of the time, I was reluctant to take people up on their offers to do things with them or to take their offers of help. Though I believe I got better at this during my father's illness, I'd like to suggest that you open your heart and allow other people to help you. They may feel helpless or feel bad for you, seeing you in such pain and so tense. This is hard on them, too. If there are offers to help, know that it's not a critique of your process. It's a gift; it's an offering of a soft pillow to fall on.

Offers of help or kindness have many potential sources, and it's okay to take advantage of them. I had many gestures of support. Social workers, housekeeping, even food service people would reach out. *Would you like a juice?* or, *Can I get you something?* or, *Let me bring you a blanket,* or, *Can I bring you a cup of tea?* Coach yourself to say yes sometimes.

The cycle of giving is such that you're not only to give, you're also to receive, and you're to show gratitude when someone else gives. I look at that as a 360° cycle. The advice I would have given myself at those times would have been to openly accept and be grateful for whatever people were trying to do to help me. Allow yourself to recognize, acknowledge, and accept help from others. This may be from those you love or others you encounter.

Also realize that you do not have to accept all offers of assistance. There are situations, people, or conversations that can leave you more drained as you navigate end-of-life issues with your loved one.

Take care of yourself by politely declining offers you suspect may drain you. I have three go-to phrases that easily extract you from these situations:

1. "Thank you very much for your offer. I will let you know if I need to take you up on that."

2. "That's a very kind offer. Thank you, but we're good for now."

3. And my favorite for people who just keep talking, "I don't mean to cut you off, but I really need go to the restroom. Please excuse me."

Keep yourself present, because there are many gifts that come up during and after somebody dies. If you're present and you can capture these gifts, holy cow! It's earth-shatteringly amazing. It re-affirms life, rather than death.

CHAPTER THREE

The Incredible Honor in the Process

UNDERSTANDING SOMEONE'S WISHES

Although I was very close with my parents, we didn't really have thorough discussions about what their wishes were. In fact, their wishes, as far as their services and burial, were not in their wills. For both of them, my sister and I had to rely on what we thought they may want, what we felt were family traditions and religious traditions and processes that felt genuine to us.

The next section explains the routes that we took to be at peace with closing this chapter on their book of life and things that you may consider as you cross that same bridge.

Decisions About My Dad's Wake and Burial

Honoring final wishes was a little bit easier for us with my dad. I had seven years with him after the death of my mom. During those seven years, I spoke with him and grew to understand how he felt about a broad variety of topics, including end-of-life concerns, much more than I had with my mom. We had even discussed what were *extraordinary measures* to keep someone alive, what would be easiest on the family, and what would be considered acceptable for him personally as well, according to his religion. In honoring him, many of the steps we took were straightforward, yet we had to make judgment calls on some aspects as his life came to a close.

My father wanted to be buried, and we already had a place for him in the cemetery where my mother was, but the process and timing were a little bit different. First, he passed away on a Sunday, and we decided to have his services delayed until Friday and Saturday. We chose this timing because family and friends were traveling from out of town, and my sister and I had kids in college with obligations that needed to be met before they could be with us. The extra days allowed us time and space in which we could breathe and move toward the wake and the services in a more controlled way and at a better pace.

A key second decision we made was to determine if we should have an open or closed casket. I went to the funeral parlor to see my father the day before to decide. I knew that he was alright with me making that decision. When I arrived at the funeral parlor, I was a bit nervous but was quickly ushered into the room where my father lay. When I saw him in the casket, it didn't look much like him, though this made the decision easier for me. His countenance was not like I knew it to be. In hindsight, I realized that the undertaker had never asked for his picture for reference.

I also recalled the last time I had seen his face after he passed away at the hospice. At that time, his face had relaxed; the labored breathing and pain was over. A look of rapture took over his face and that had filled me with joy. Here now at the funeral parlor, it didn't remind me of that beautiful experience at all, so I chose to have a closed casket.

I knew, too, that a closed casket would be easier for my sister and all the grandchildren. I remembered an exchange that took place between my dad and my sister when we had buried my father's sister, Betty. He had seen my sister's discomfort at Betty's wake and addressed it. I recall him saying to her that he knew it bothered her, and she could go into the other room. He also added that, when he passed away, it would be okay with him if the casket was closed to make it easier on her or me.

Somehow, I remembered that, maybe fifteen or twenty years later, and used both of those memories as a reference point. I later learned that my father's brother, Ray, was also worried about the fact that it might be an open casket and was totally relieved when it wasn't. Instead, we used beautiful pictures as a way to remember my father. It made a lot of sense, and it created much more of a celebration of life, which was what we all wanted for that ceremony.

Decisions About My Mom's Wake and Burial

When we were incorporating The News that my mother was, in fact, going to be passing on, we had to take care of a few things. The first thing was determining where we were going to bury her. Interestingly enough, although my parents were both in their eighties, they had not chosen a burial plot. My sister and I relied on my dad for this decision, and he suggested a cemetery that had advertised in the church bulletin. We made an appointment, then went there together to look at things. The cemetery didn't feel right to me, but I chose to keep my feelings quiet to be supportive of my father. My impression was that it felt more like a parking lot than a peaceful cemetery. Everything was ordered, all the plots and headstones were the same size, there was a mausoleum; it felt very impersonal to me. My dad decided to choose a plot in the mausoleum; he thought it would be good to be able to get out of the weather, if needed, when we went to visit her there.

I had supported his decision but, behind the scenes, I tried to find a better option. In my heart, the choice didn't feel right. I made some phone calls when I was in the bathroom at the hospital or when I was at home and people couldn't hear me. I felt the need to keep my dissention to myself as things were already rough. Through my secretive efforts, I was able to find what I thought might be a good option. I still was not ready to bring this forward to my dad and sister, but it was difficult to make an excuse to get away from them. So, I shorted out the blow dryer, which gave me an excuse to go to the pharmacy to purchase a new one. In fact, I was going to check out this potential new burial space.

Finding this new cemetery was such beautiful synchronicity. The staff had just reviewed their deeds and found several plots that were still available. It was a beautiful cemetery with trees and flowers; it felt more like a beautiful garden in many ways, like what I knew my parents loved. This whole process of seeking, especially in secret, felt strange to me; I found the whole idea of being proactive on matters surrounding death *wrong*. I didn't want to be *caught* doing it. Strangely, it felt like something I should hide. That changed once I visited this place; in my heart, if felt right.

When I returned home from the cemetery visit, I sat down with my father and sister, and said, "I don't want you to feel like I'm being unsupportive, but I have found another option for Mom for us to consider. It's much closer, and it seems to be a bit more of a happy and peaceful place. If you're willing, I'd like to take you there."

They were, so we went. Everything fell into place easily and quickly. Both of them really loved the place, so we cancelled our prior arrangements and secured a plot at this cemetery. Afterwards, my dad thanked me and said I should have never worried about voicing my thoughts.

You may not know what your loved one's wishes are, or things may not be predetermined, but by giving yourself some time, you can find a better outcome. Take a breath, be present, check in with yourself and what you are feeling. When approached with care and love, you may be able to offer or find options that are acceptable to the family when your loved one hasn't given clear guidance.

Having the Courage to Initiate Conversations About Death

It is helpful to realize that open conversations about death and final wishes are actually a loving thing to do. It's a way to give the people who are left behind a path to follow, to feel comfortable about their decisions, because some of the decisions are pre-arranged or predetermined. It's also important to understand that some people are ambivalent or do not want to make decisions regarding their final wishes. Ironically, for my mom and dad, they really didn't have many of those discussions, even though they were in their eighties, had dealt with the deaths of many family members, and even had a health crisis or two.

The only discussion I recalled with my mother was one where she said, "Oh, just cremate me. I don't care."

This single reference, though, was discarded. Because her passing came as the result of burns, we couldn't even consider that. Additionally, this was not common in our family, mainly due to traditions and religious beliefs at the time.

My dad and I worked through some of our grief together after my mom died. Many times when I'd visit, we would prepare a nice dinner and share a bottle of wine or two. It really opened a lot of doors for conversations to explore what was acceptable, what was preferred. He was at peace with being able to speak about this.

He always pulled two wine glasses out. His was from one of his retirement lunches and had an inscription, "You wine, I'll listen."

I loved that. He was such a great listener and sounding board for me. He could easily handle my intensity and passion in a loving and helpful way. I find myself, now, having some of those discussions with my husband and children. It's not all written down in detail yet, but there are some clear headlines and topics which I know will help guide them through that. At times, they've even inserted into the conversation their own wishes, which I respect and find comforting. Maybe, perhaps as I get older, I'll be putting those down on paper, too.

Emotions keep many people from having these discussions, though emotions naturally come with the realization that the two of you are going to permanently, physically separate. The emotions arise because you are jumping to the future, and you predict the feelings you will have when the other dies. These feelings, now or when the death occurs, are unavoidable. And the tears that may come are evidence of the deep love that you feel for each other. It's okay to allow these emotions, to experience them because, in the end, it's about love. The journey through the emotions leads to guidance on how to oversee that final honor. You are enabled to lay a loved one to rest in a way that feels respectful of their wishes and respectful of yours.

An additional benefit of these preemptive discussions is that it frees you from some worries and concerns, so you can be more present for the emotions you feel when the death occurs. These discussions don't have to be all at once; perhaps just a question or two here and there. It could be a one-on-one conversation or in a group. Seize opportunities to ask a question or two — opportunities arise frequently. Perhaps they come up when someone close passes away; perhaps when a celebrity passes on. Capture these opportunities. Take the risk of bringing it up, perhaps piece by piece.

CHANGING THE PROCESS OF DEATH FROM A FEARFUL OR TABOO-RIDDEN EXPERIENCE TO A CELEBRATION

Many emotions and circumstances can arise when you're in the process of losing someone. It's easy to be stuck in your head and not be present for what is actually happening. As a result, you can miss out on opportunities to make this process more fulfilling or complete. As my sister and I were losing our parents, we chose to do some things for the sole purpose of having *something to do*. Following are a few stories about some of the activities we found to be helpful, either for us or, we hoped, for our mom and dad. I believe some of these really made a difference.

Things Which May Make It Easier for the Ill or Dying Person

A common misconception about people who are passing away — in particular, those who can no longer communicate — is that they may not be sensing what is going on in the room. Though it has not been scientifically proven, it is believed that hearing may be the last sense to go. Based upon this belief, and the possibility that they may even open their eyes, we chose to put several things in place for our parents to possibly connect with in their room. The first thing we did was to bring in a source of music. This was something my sister initiated with our mother. During her five-week stay in the burn unit, we switched between different types of music — joyful, classical, jazz, piano music; we thought the music would be soothing and help to mute out the sound of the equipment, alarms, and bells that were common in her room. When our dad moved to hospice, we immediately incorporated music.

My sister connected with our mom through touch. She suggested that we continue to touch her in a reassuring way. Due to burns and grafting surgeries, there was much of our mom that we could not touch, but her feet and her lower legs weren't impacted, so we were able to massage them with lotion. As some of the minor burns healed, we were able to include her hands in this process. With our dad, we were not as restricted. We were able to hold his hands and even help the nurses with turning him, brushing his hair, or moistening his lips or mouth. Our parents both knew that my sister and I were the ones administering this care and that we were there with them.

Once my father was moved to hospice, I felt strongly about having a candle in the room. Due to oxygen in the room, we were unable to light a candle, but the Reverend was able to provide some LED candles. To me, it made the room feel like we were holding a very sacred space for my dad.

There were times when, despite the music, he became quite agitated. The staff was ready to provide Ativan (benzodiazepine) for anxiety but, at times, I chose instead to do some guided meditations with him, knowing that my father was open to this.

Reading was a passion of my dad's and, during his hospice process, I read interesting books, in addition to occasionally reading the newspaper. When I found different things that I thought might be of interest to him, I would sit on his bed, hold his hand, and read aloud to him, in the hopes that he heard.

I assumed that there was plenty my parents were focusing on and thinking about as they moved toward their transition, but I also felt they might still have interest in some earthly things that might even spur some interesting memories or thoughts for them.

The Brochures on Dying—My Initial, Then Evolved, Perspective

I know when I say, "Change the process from one of grieving to one of celebration," this might sound crazy.

Celebration brings to mind a wedding or a birthday for many. In this instance, I am referring more to a celebration of someone's life, but also a celebration in that they are moving on to a different reality. I believe the consciousness survives physical death. When I was in hospice with my dad, the nurses spoke about the process of death as the reverse of birth. Indeed, there are many similarities. A lot of excitement builds when someone is pregnant and expecting a child. The next, natural step is the process of labor, in most cases. On the other side of that experience, there is a beautiful soul who joins our world through a new physical body.

Death is similar to that, but in reverse. For natural death, there is also a laboring process, and at the end of it, the expected outcome is physical and clinical death.

And, although it is the death of the physical body, it is also the release of the consciousness or soul.

In contemplating this, I tried to think about how I could view this time and process as a celebration for all that he had lived through, for the experiences he had that enriched his soul. Imagine how you might feel after observing a fantastic gymnastics routine or moving musical performance. This is the celebration of which I speak.

When in hospice, they had many resources for us to use. They provided two brochures that discussed the process of a person dying. One was focused on the physical signs of death—everything from changes in the breathing, their urinary output, mottling of their skin or the darkening of their nails. The other brochure focused more on the spiritual aspect of dying, and the things that would happen. When they first gave me these brochures, it blew my mind. I found them really affronting. I wanted to know about them, but I didn't want to read them.

Strangely enough, more than anything, I did not want anyone seeing me read them. I don't know that I can really explain why, but when anyone would come into the room, even my sister, I would always have another book that I was reading which I used to cover the brochure, or I would discreetly tuck it back in my bag or something. I felt like I shouldn't be caught reading this—kind of like how you might feel if your parents caught you reading pornography. They were truly helpful, and I can only think these feelings were about my inner conflict of knowing he was dying and consciously accepting that fact. My conscious mind was still rejecting this reality, even though I appeared fully engaged in the hospice process. It is amazing how denial can show up.

I had mentioned the brochures to my sister and, at one point, my sister asked for them. I handed them over—relieved in a sense, like we now shared a similar vice. Only then did it dawn on me how helpful they were for me, and that they could be helpful to others. I later discussed this with a friend whose mother had passed away quickly. She had similar feelings, but also found the brochures to be useful as a way to move forward, a *How To*. It also felt *wrong* to check my father for some of the physical symptoms I read about. Over time, I became slightly more open with that. The nurses saw this and then also became more open with tracking those physical signs of death with me as well.

When my mom was passing away, I did not have the brochures, and I did not know anything about the physical signs of death, so I was ignorant to the tracking of symptoms. There was one thing that I was deeply curious and concerned about, and asked a nurse about it. Years back, my mom had a valve replaced in her heart and a pacemaker put in. Though we were told her heart rate would slow down and eventually stop at the end of her life, I asked what would happen with the pacemaker. Would it still try to make her heart start? What would happen? Something about her dying and the pacemaker still trying to beat frightened me. I was given an interesting answer: the heart does stop and the pacemaker can't restart it. When she died, they would be able to shut it off with a magnet they placed on her chest. It felt strange asking the question, but I felt comforted knowing that there would not be any kind of drama at the end of her life, and it would still be a peaceful passing.

If you have questions at any point, find the courage to ask. Having an answer is far better than fantasizing about one.

Birthing Into a New World, a New Reality

My experience of losing my mom was very different than that of losing my dad. With my mom's death, I was still caught up in the fear of losing her and the feelings of loss. I was both focused on not missing her death and my fear of what life would be without my mom. Though her death spurred a period of major spiritual growth, during those five weeks in the hospital when we knew she would die, I did not realize I wasn't being present. I was focused on fixing her and then being with her when she died.

When my father went into hospice, both the coaching of the staff and the experience of my mom passing first helped me be more prepared, open, and present. I gravitated to the idea presented to me—that death is like birth in reverse with many similarities. The consciousness, or soul, was birthing into the next reality. Through the support staff and brochures and books on dying I was reading at the time, I was able to come to peace with the idea that this is a process, and it will take as long as it takes, like labor and delivery.

Each day became not so much about, *Will it happen? It was more, Where are we in the process? What's happening today?*

Being more conscious, and not being as fearful of *when* he passed, made it better for me. I helped myself see: *These are the steps. These are the things that are happening along the way.*

Though I rarely left my father's side during the two weeks in hospice, my desire to be present was more to be there to support him and witness his journey.

When you are approaching the birth of a child, in particular, for the first time, certainly there's a lot of excitement but there are also fears.

You may find yourself asking lots of questions: *Will the baby be okay? Will I be okay? Will there be a lot of pain? Will it be a lot of drama? Will it go okay? Will it happen on time? Will it be early? Will it be late?*

When I reflect on those thoughts, they are similar to what you think about when somebody is passing away, as I've mentioned before.

Is it possible that, through viewing it in this manner, we can perhaps shift death into something that is positive?

It cracks open the door to honor the process and allow for a more fulfilling and less fearful experience.

I recognize that beliefs around life, death, and the afterlife can be different. Not everyone believes in heaven or hell, or reincarnation, or life after death, or the continuation of a soul or consciousness. Despite these differing beliefs, I feel that the concept of birthing into a new reality still applies, even when one has atheistic or agnostic beliefs.

If, for you, the concept doesn't seem to apply because you do not believe that the soul continues, perhaps, at the least, it applies to *you* when you lose someone. You are the one birthing into a new part of *your* life. The person who dies will no longer be physically present in your life. They *will* be present in your mind, in your pictures, and in your heart, but they will no longer be physically there. This concept of physically birthing into a new reality then applies to you.

HONORING THE DEATH AND BURIAL PROCESS

I would like to share a few stories from my personal journey of my parents' passing. These events stand out in my mind as milestones as I moved through these times. There was tremendous richness in that process, not only in the traditions or rituals, but also in specific little events that were steps along the way for closure for me, and perhaps for the rest of my family as well.

Memorials, Burials, and Final Goodbyes

When we first approached this, there seemed to be a certain structure around the steps and stages of what had to be done:

- Who was going to write the obituary?
- What was going into the obituary?
- What things had to happen in services?
- What was going to be done at the grave site?

There were many things, some easy to see, some required, but there were many places for us to personalize. We could not personalize at the church; they did not allow laypeople to offer a eulogy, which was both worrisome and relieving to me. I was fairly sure I knew what to say, yet was also quite sure that my delivery would include long gaps to quiet my emotions, so that I could continue speaking. For our mom's service, I provided the priest with two writings that I had hoped would prepare him to eulogize our mom well. One of them was a letter, several pages long, that I had written to my mother, titled, "What I Love About My Mom."

She was always telling me that she didn't want anything for Mothers' Day, so one year, instead of purchasing a gift, I captured in a letter all these beautiful memories I had of her and how much I had felt her support throughout my life. She had loved it and luckily, we still had it. The other document was the one I had prepared to help her caregivers know more about her, "A Bit About Magdalen Martha Pitel O'Boyle."

During her eulogy, I found it quite unsettling that the priest referred to these documents, even waved them while he spoke, but delivered none of their content. He also got her name wrong, calling her Madelyn. I was glad that I had thought to provide these to the funeral home so they were, at least, displayed to be read by guests there.

When it came time for my dad's funeral, I was clear about my expectations with the priest in our planning meeting and made it very clear that I wanted certain things to be spoken about. The priest delivered a beautiful, heartfelt eulogy, and I was happy he honored my dad well. Irrespective of where a service is held, personalized eulogies offer such a welcomed touch to the service. Taking care in selecting the speakers and setting guidelines or expectations can help ensure your wishes are addressed here as well.

I'd also like to add a tip from a friend on delivering a eulogy: it is not possible to drink water and cry at the same time. Have a glass of water handy while delivering your speech and, when the tears begin to arise, take a drink and you will both center yourself and stop the tears. *Thanks, Cathy!* More recently, photos and videos have become quite common as a visual eulogy; our extended family has developed and shared cherished videos that combine memories from a broad cross section of photo collections — many of which contain photos that evoke laughter and fun memories.

Preparing an obituary was a bit more straightforward for our mother because our father was still with us and knew and contributed most of the information. When our father passed, I made sure that I spoke to several people in his family to ensure information they might have was included. It reflected the respect and honor they had for him as well. I learned in this process, from my Uncle Ray, that my dad had been a *Wonder Boy*.

After high school, he tested well when he volunteered for the Air Force and was enlisted in OCS, an accelerated program to become a commissioned officer. He then went to flight school and became a pilot. This was a great source of pride to his family, and he was a bit of a hometown hero. My dad had only spoken about signing up and becoming a pilot. He had not spoken about these details, and I was proud to learn about them.

This led to another profound moment for me. I was taking the lead on most of the arrangements with the funeral parlor, and I thought I had gotten everything right. Personally, I was hesitant to have the full military burial. I had witnessed this at the burial of my Uncle Joe, and it was beautiful but really rocked me — the playing of "Taps," the salute, the folding and presentation of the flag to the family. Wow. Those fears led to my hesitancy, but, when I mentioned it to my sister, that was one thing that she really wanted. She also felt that his family would want that, too. So, we added a full military burial.

I believed I managed well enough the day of the funeral up until we got to the cemetery. As we entered the grounds and walked to the grave site, I saw the Honor Guard there. I immediately choked up, but I knew that it would be a beautiful service. They had played "Taps," conducted the salute, and folded the flag. After they folded the flag, they looked for whom they should present the flag to, and I gestured to my sister, being that she was the oldest. She accepted the flag with composure I never could have mastered, with such strength and respect. She then turned and walked over to my son—the only grandson—and handed the flag to him. He accepted it with poise and honor. I watched this in awe, and was deeply touched by it. I was truly glad we did it and made no attempt to halt the river of tears that flowed as a result.

Later that day, Jack, a dear friend of my husband's and mine, came back to my father's house with a gift for my son. He had purchased a display case for the flag from the military burial.

Jack handed that to our son and said, "Now, you can really preserve that flag and put it in a place of honor in your home."

To this day, it sits on our fireplace mantle. And, of course, I lost my composure again at that point. I later learned of a loving and kind conversation he had with our daughter while my dad was in hospice. We were blessed to have family and friends that circled us during this tough time in simple yet profound ways.

Getting the Word Out and Capturing Contact Information

Obituaries are useful to communicate The News beyond your inner circle; they are also a key tool to convey information about services. Writing one is important, but getting it out where people can access it is necessary. If your loved one worked in a different area, lived in a distant community or several communities over their life, or they were raised in a different area, do your best to try to place obituaries in newspapers that service those other areas. Also, attempt to connect with people they had gone to school with or worked with in the past, and old friends, so that the word gets around. It allows the information to flow to people that they may have lost touch with but may want to reconnect as they passed away. It also may offer opportunities for you to connect with your loved one in a new way through the stories they share. Social media is also a tool to get the word out and is more mainstream now.

I was a bit surprised at both wakes and services by some of the people who showed up—old acquaintances, people who knew my parents but not me. Most times at a wake or service, a guest book is set out capture who came. I found that useful when it came time to send thank-you notes.

If you are a guest at visiting hours or anywhere a guest book is present, please sign it, fully and legibly. It is used by the family as a list for sending thank-you notes and as a reminder of everyone who came. Those times can be a blur, and this record is important to stay in touch both in the near future and in the long term.

We were grateful for the reminder. That book doesn't tend to get misplaced, and it is a way for these reconnections to continue. I have cousins I have not seen in ages, yet we enjoyed time together when we were growing up. It would be nice to still stay in touch. Completing that entry helps.

There were also many people who offered a cell phone number or email to either my sister or me, and we captured the information on random pieces of paper. Much was going on and frankly, much of it was a blur. These papers tended to get misplaced, and we lost a bunch of information. I did not think to have my own book there by my side where I could capture these email addresses or cell phone numbers.

My word of advice would be to have another book, maybe sitting on your chair with a pen attached to it, so that you can capture when folks offer an email address or phone number. That way, it is all in one place for you. The small pieces of paper will get lost. Another option is to have the guest registry customized to capture this along with the guest information. It was unfortunate connections were lost, but I'm hoping this preempts that for others.

The Experience of the Funeral Home

You are quite fortunate if you have a funeral director who is warm, compassionate, and skilled at walking you through this process. As I helped navigate my family through the process, it was my first time in this role and the first time I had ever been a part of the process. There was quite a lot that I did not know, and there were quite a few things that I was very hesitant to ask. One of these things, and this sounds crazy, was around clothing—they ask you to bring clothes for your loved one to be buried in.

Yikes! What do you bring?

It's not about what's on the outside—for sure, that takes consideration, but it is familiar ground. So, do you also bring hosiery? Underwear? What exactly does *clothing* mean?

I had to ask and the answer was, "Whatever you feel is appropriate."

I went on a tangent and thought about the breadth of possibilities. I know that there are some traditions where the family actually washes then clothes the body. There are others that clothe their loved ones in a simple gown, like at baptism.

Coming back to my situation, I thought: *You know what? You put all of her clothes on her, and do everything to treat that body with respect.* In my eyes, the body of a loved one is special. Although it doesn't hold the soul, consciousness, or essence of the person anymore, their body represents a special and particular vehicle through which God chose to show his love for you — through that person. Honoring their body, and treating it with such incredible reverence, respect, and love is vital. I realized that you simply do what you feel is right. I imagine there are similar considerations with cremation or when a body cannot be recovered.

I had thought I navigated that one well, but was unprepared for the next set of questions upon bringing my mother's clothing to the funeral home.

These valid yet awkward questions were fielded next:

- Do you want her jewelry back?
- Do you want her rosaries back?
- Do you want to keep the crucifix from the coffin?

And several more, I'm sure. There's the shock of the question, there's the awkward response, and then there is the internal question: *What do I do with that stuff when I get it back?*

My mind went to some new places with some of those thoughts. It was yet another area I was simply not prepared for, yet they were valid questions. They served to jar me back into the present. After a brief, internal, tumultuous few moments, I came to the rational conclusion that she was not going to need those things anymore. The soul does not need material goods.

I responded that yes, we did want them back. Although I must admit, on the drive back home, I was still in a bit of shock after this combined with the clothing question.

This series of questions continued. When we returned to the funeral home, prior to the service on the day of her funeral, I was again asked about the jewelry — did we want my mom's earrings back?

I was so jolted into the present and shocked by it, that I responded, "Let me get back to you on that."

I then quickly retreated to the ladies' room. This question caused me to realize that all her possessions were no longer necessary for her; she wasn't going to need them anymore. She really was gone. It was another true representation to me that she was *gone,* in the physical sense, from my life. I needed a moment. I needed to be alone and cry it out.

After a few minutes, I came back out and said, "Yes, I will take those back." It would be something of hers that we could pass on to either me or my sister, or our girls.

Similar questions came up as we went through the process for my dad. I was far better prepared and conscious that the questions would come, and I felt much more confident in my responses. The questions for him were asked about his wedding band and his watch at the hospice upon his death and, this time, I chose differently. Ever since my mother had passed away, he never chose to take his wedding band off. The nurse asked if I wanted his ring or his watch. I said that yes, I would take his watch, but no, I wanted to leave his wedding band on.

Again, at the funeral parlor, they asked me if I wanted his wedding band. To me, because he had chosen not to take it off in those seven years of separation since her death, it actually felt right for that to go with him as he joined her in their burial site. The watch was different. My father always wore watches, and he was fond of the ones that were atomic-clock set. He still wore his watch all through his hospitalization and hospice. It was still counting time after his life ended.

When I told this story, my niece expressed interest in it and became its new owner. My father's brother,

Bob, also had a fondness of watches, and he and my niece spoke a bit about them at the repass dinner. Bob, too, gave her one of his own watches. My dad was the second oldest and first son in his family; Uncle Bob was the youngest of eight and the youngest son. Something felt really right about the transfer of timekeeping to the youngest generation of our family. I loved this.

The Gift of Selecting My Dad's Burial Clothes

There is yet another story about the clothing in preparation for the funeral. When it came time for me to select clothes for my father to be buried in, I first looked for his dress shoes. He hadn't worn them in a while, though my father was of the generation who embraced those classic wing-tipped shoes. I found the perfect black pair in his closet, but they were a little dusty. I recalled that he had a shoeshine kit downstairs. He used the shoeshine kit for his shoes and mine. Whenever I left out leather shoes during a visit, he would take them and shine them for me. He believed it was very important to leave a good impression coming and going, and shoes were a part of that.

"If you walk out of a room, the last thing someone sees is the back of your shoes; you've got to make sure that they're all shined up and not nicked on the back from driving the car!"

The memory gave me strength to pull the shoes out and shine them one last time for him, but the house was still in disarray from the carpeting and there was no place for me to easily set up to do this. So, I took the kit and my dad's shoes and sat on the front porch of his house, polishing them. It was such an honorable process for me. I now think back and conjure that image, which comforts me.

I went back inside to choose a suit, shirt, and tie, from his days as a corporate employee. I selected a stately black single-breasted suit and began going through the pants and jacket pockets. When I slipped my hand into the outside right pocket of his jacket, I found a couple of tissues. It brought me right back to all those times that I went to the funerals of family members with my dad. Inevitably, during those funerals, there always came a time when the tears start to flow for me, and I could never seem to get to my purse or tissues fast enough. My dad was always quick to pull a tissue or two from his pocket, having it ready-at-hand for me. I cannot say how comforting it was to find, that even after he passed, there was a tissue in his pocket, still waiting for me. I took it out, breathed in his scent deeply and used it. The gentlest sense of gratitude and the knowing that he would always, somehow, be with me flooded over me through my tears.

These final processes, acts, or steps that you take in laying to rest a loved one can be helpful to you as you come to terms with your loss and grief. I found it valuable to view every action as a way to honor my mother and father. This view served to help me keep my perspective and also pulled me into the present and grounded me. It grounded me such that my emotions did not paralyze me, rather, it held me in a very solid place of action, honoring their memory but not focusing on the loss alone.

After weeks of being trapped in a holding pattern, of waiting for them to get better or pass away, it gave me tremendous strength to take action during this process. I recall sharing this vivid personal truth with several friends upon the loss of their parents and responding to their desperation of loss with the advice of taking action and finding the strength to honor their parent and the process in their own way.

Cherish whatever it is that you have the opportunity to take part in. These are the last acts that you can take for your loved one. In the case in which someone has provided input for their service before they passed, I imagine this too can provide comfort as you follow the roadmap they left for you. Try to look at it as something that you actually *can do* versus getting all bunched up and tense. Whatever process emerges for your final services, know that each step of it slowly moves you along the path to accepting their death and moving forward again in your life. I found tremendous comfort in that, and I hope others can as well.

It's all an exploration of love, even if there is contention surrounding the passing. The incredible emotions you go through, the thoughts and feelings death evokes are powerful, dynamic, and catalytic. I'd like to think that the emotional explorations are a testament that this person lives on in the love that you carry in your heart.

THE HONOR IN RESOLVING WHAT THEY'VE LEFT BEHIND

When somebody dies, they no longer need anything that was a part of their earthly existence. Their things, though, can mean quite a bit to those who are left behind. *Things* become something to hold onto, something to help create memories, and perhaps a way in which the person lives on. There is almost a clash resulting between these two points; one no longer needs it, and the other may still be holding on. Your process of managing or resolving the things and situations left behind can really help you in your process of grieving and moving on in positive ways.

Take the Time to Go Through Things, If You Can

My parents had lived in the same home for almost fifty-five years. As a result of sharing life together for all that time, there was a ton of things left behind, a ton of memories. When my mother passed away, seven years before my father did, he chose to leave her things intact. There were a few pieces of jewelry that we gave to the granddaughters, but other than that, everything of my mom's remained in place. When my dad passed away, we then had the challenge of going through his things and my mom's. It was a daunting task and we decided to take our time in doing this. There were no pressing time or finance-sensitive reasons that required us to move quickly.

My sister and I differed in our opinions on the approach to take. I'm more of a collector than she is; she is excellent at organization. Between our styles, we were able to arrive at a compromise to get it done. Our process took longer because of my need for time, but also because neither of us lived nearby. As a result, it took about a year and a half for the house to be fully emptied and sold.

How Amazing It Feels to Gift Things

We did not have an opportunity to ask our mother what her thoughts were about her possessions, but with our father, I did have that chance. During a visit with him at rehab, he commented that he felt bad that my sister and I would have a lot to go through. I told him not to worry about it, but then asked if he had any thoughts or wishes about his things. He had told me that he really didn't care much about anything, but he did have a couple of collections — his books and his tools. As I paced myself when going through the house, I tried to go fairly quickly but did leave the tools and the books more to the end, so that I could savor his collections. As I went through his books, I marveled at the similarities in our interests while putting together piles of books for different grandchildren, for myself, for friends. The rest were donated, not disposed of.

Our mom had small collections of crystal, Lenox china, jewelry, and tons of pictures. The granddaughters took some things they treasured. There was a neighbor who was also one of Mom's dear friends. Mom had helped her with meals and long conversations as Pat went through two bouts of breast cancer. They were close. Two beautiful vases found their new home with Pat.

I brought them over to her filled with roses from my mother's garden and said, "I really think that my mom would love for you to have these."

She was honored and happy and cleared a space on her table for them. When I returned on trips to clean out the house, I used to bring flowers over for her to put in those vases. I know we both really treasured these moments, and her warm, loving hugs always reminded me of my mom.

Another neighbor who kindly kept an eye on my dad helped me rehome a bedroom set, which delighted a little girl; and she found a home for a vase that I'm sure reminds her of Mom. Her husband, who my dad helped with various house needs, kindly accepted some ladders.

There were even Christmas decorations that went to different relatives; my cousins and I had great memories of our Christmases growing up together. There was a beautiful china cabinet that my mother cherished. When cousins came to help me with clean out, one of them fell in love with it and was thrilled she got to keep that piece in the family, along with some antique Christmas ornaments. The china cabinet went back to Pennsylvania, along with some furniture and lamps that also were appreciated. Almost as a reward for plowing through all this stuff, my cousins Ginny and Cheryl and I enjoyed divvying up the contents of the bar, as well as sharing a cocktail or two in the process. All this helped make that weekend productive and joyful.

Many of my dad's tools were very old, but I wanted our son to have some of them because he is the sole grandson. My husband and a friend went to the house and chose a bunch of them, so that our son could have these as part of his first set of tools. That was really special to me because of my father's wishes and the continuity it brought. Our son also has my dad's Air Force dress uniform and medals.

Our daughter was in college during this time, and we knew soon she'd move out on her own, so we saved the everyday plates, my mother's china, recipe books, baking and cookware, and silverware for her. When my daughter moved to her first apartment, she was able to start off with some familiar things and reduce her initial expenses, thanks to her grandmother. Ironically, I texted her on the tenth anniversary of my mom's passing, a bit sad, and she responded with joy as she was enjoying this reconnection. She even texted pictures of handwritten recipes from my mom's cookbooks she was perusing. Such a beautiful, full circle event for us.

We gave our father's car to a friend who is a veteran. We loved that we found a home for it with a veteran connection. On its ride to its new home in Vermont, it actually bumped into and knocked over a moose . . . without damage to the small car. Wow. I fancied that my dad had protected it and its new owner. Although the moose was knocked over by the car, he got back up and trotted into the woods.

There are many things to consider when going through belongings. It felt wonderful to give things away, knowing that it created a beautiful space or memory in someone else's home. There were however, many things that had lost value, were out of style, or were not donatable. There was also a ton of paperwork that was no longer needed. In hindsight, I did not understand that my inability to rehome or sell things was a sign of this lack of value. I was also opposed to a house sale, but now see that it could have expedited the process and perhaps saved many things from being disposed of.

We wanted to preserve my mother's garden. My mom was an amazing gardener and absolutely adored roses and flowers. I spent a lot of time digging flowers out of her garden and bringing them up to my garden in Vermont. I remember buying top soil, digging holes, and trying to get flowers in every time I would return home with a bunch. I adamantly wanted to transfer this beauty to my garden, even digging the flowers in one time as the light was fading and it was starting to snow. Seeing them come up and bloom the next spring delighted my heart. My sister and my cousin Ginny also have beautiful gardens, and we are hoping that several of my mother's rosebushes will take for them. So, it's not only objects and furniture, it can also be living things like plants or pets and the feeling they create.

Packing Their Bags

When I started to go through my parents' clothes, I had my cousins and my friend there helping me. We were running out of bags and boxes to put them in when I remembered that there were a bunch of suitcases upstairs. This sounds kind of crazy, but it was something that I kind of felt good about. I pulled together some of these suitcases for pieces of the beautiful dress clothes and coats of my parents and folded them nicely, as if they were going on a trip. There was something kind of complete about doing that for me. It felt a bit like I was sending them away on probably the best journey of their soul — maybe back together again. The next week, I put the full suitcases out on the front porch for the Disabled American Veterans pickup, but I imagined it was as if they were waiting for a limo to pick them up.

It felt good while I was setting things out, but as I left later that morning for work, I remember while driving away, I turned around and saw all that on the front porch, waiting for that truck. It made me sad, for many reasons. I decided to just take a picture. When I looked at it afterwards, it was beautiful; beams of sunshine streaked the image. The picture made me feel better, like it was an acknowledgement of my parents saying *It's okay.*

The Gift of Reviewing Correspondence

My parents were from the generation that wrote letters in script to keep in touch. Mom had beautiful handwriting. I found it a thoughtful, beautiful thing to do and enjoyed seeing that other people had kept in touch with her this way, too. As I went through their things, I found many letters and evidence of this love of writing and communication style.

There was a beautiful old letter from the 1950s. My mother had written to someone and asked for a cake recipe she enjoyed during a visit. The woman had written back to her, honored that she wanted the recipe and took care in hand-writing the recipe. Beautiful. There were other letters saved that told of family members who had passed away. Another friend had taken the time to cut out an obituary and include it in a letter for them.

My dad's letter collection was more eclectic, with letters from a variety of sources. He kept thank-you letters from neighbors. During his morning walks, he would put people's newspapers in between their doors, put their garbage cans out, or find ways to give people a helping hand. In return, neighbors would leave him a little St. Patty's Day present, like Irish soda bread with a cute card or a letter of gratitude. He saved many of these, and I loved reading them. It demonstrated a beautiful circle of gratitude and caring.

Perhaps they helped him ease the pain and disconnection he felt when my mom died. There was a letter from a gentleman that was written to my father when both men were in their eighties; it was about a woman who was apparently the source of a disagreement when they were in their thirties. I found it amazing that after over fifty years had passed, there was a letter seeking to straighten that out.

There were a ton of letters written by my cousin Edie Ann; she faithfully kept him in touch with her mom, Aunt Claire, as her mother's sight had failed. The letters were filled with beautiful handwriting, careful thoughts, and discussion about the family. My father kept each of them. He treasured and valued that connection to his family.

There was a set of heart-stopping letters that I had found, ones that my father had written to my mother after she had passed away. He had written about three or four of them, on different occasions like my mother's birthday, Christmas, their anniversary, or Valentine's Day. In them, he shared how much he had missed her and, despite the help of loved ones or his faith in God, he still missed her dearly and longed for the time when they would be together again. They were such beautiful yet simple love letters to her after she had gone.

If I had not taken the time to go through all the correspondence, I would have missed some of these unbelievable treasures. Though many brought tears to my eyes, most left me tremendously grateful for the people who took the time to do more than just sign a card to genuinely share, to keep in touch. With many families far flung, we can lose touch with relationships. It was reassuring to see how many kept in touch with my parents.

The Gift of Help: Everyone Benefits

The first time we started going through the house, it was my sister, my son, and I. It was kind of fun, and there was a camaraderie that developed between my sister and son as they set aside items to place out at the curb for others to take. We wanted to think that maybe there would be a home for them. If not, the garbage service would take them in the morning.

Other times, two of my cousins helped me. That was amazing, because there were many things that were still in our family that reminded us of the times we were all growing up together—something as simple as hand-made doilies stitched by my mother and her sisters. We had similar Christmas ornaments. We had ornaments that were from our grandmother's tree that we all recalled. We remembered times we had gone shopping for deals after Christmas, to buy new balls or new lights for the trees. It was nice to be able to share that.

Sometimes we'd have a drink and share a good laugh about it, too. One time when they were there, we were trying to figure out who was going to sleep where, because some of the furniture had been given away. One of my cousins said she was okay with sleeping in my parents' bedroom, which I had never done and was not comfortable doing. Though I worried, she was fine and had no strange dreams. When she arose and went to the bathroom the next morning, she found a pair of black gloves lying on the bed when she returned to the room. She didn't remember them being there before she went to sleep, so she mentioned it afterwards.

She said, "Whose gloves were these on my bed?"

We looked and we said, "Oh, they're not mine! They're not mine."

Then I said, "You know, those are the gloves my father used to put on before he used to rewind the grandfather clock and move it."

We all kind of joked and thought that maybe my dad had placed them on there because we were moving parts of the grandfather clock, and we were doing it with our bare hands. As the oils on your hands can really impact how it can work or the brass finish, we kind of thought that was funny.

We were thinking that maybe that was a sign from my dad to say, "Watch it when you move that grandfather clock! Treat it with respect, and use gloves."

We had a lot of fun laughs about that, too.

My friend helped me through a lot. As we went through my mom's knickknacks, silver, crystal, and things, it really brought up a lot of the different times in her life when she remembered times with her grandmother and her mother, leading to some very deep and rich discussions about what we think about when people die and how it was for each of us. We had a lot of healing and revealing conversations in a very positive way.

The presence and assistance of family and friends was enriching and therapeutic for me. This was yet another gift I experienced during my grief.

Going Through Family Bibles

My daughter had reminded me that she wanted bibles from my mother. My parents seemed to have quite a collection of both prayer books and bibles, so I was trying to go through those, to think which ones might be the ones to give to her. Some had prayer cards from other people's wakes past tucked in them, some printed prayers, and so on.

Upon opening one, I noted there were two dates in the front of the Bible. I believe one was in April, and the other in October. My mom, although she came from a big family, had some trouble having children. She suffered both a miscarriage and a stillbirth before she had my sister and I. We talked a little bit about that. I knew that the stillborn baby was a boy. We had visited his grave. I knew that I had reminded her of him, but I never knew much about the dates. When I asked my mom's sisters about this, they didn't know very much. It was one of those hush-hush things that wasn't spoken about much.

Just seeing those two dates reminded me of how much those events must have meant to my mother, and I was grateful for the small amount of conversation that we had had about those. I wished I had been able to talk to her more about those and maybe even help her complete some more healing on them. As a mother, I now longed to know more. I had many questions to ask her, yet there would be no answers. I now assume those two dates are respectively the dates of her miscarried and stillborn children.

Dad also had a few bibles, one had been given to him by his mother. It had the birth dates of everyone in his immediate family clearly noted inside. My father was one of eight children, so there were ten dates. As people passed away in the family, he made it one of his rituals to record the date that they had passed away. I reconnected with this bible when going through his books and realized, as I looked at the list, that it was time for me to complete his entry, to record his date of death next to his birth date. I poured myself a nice glass of wine, said a prayer, then sat down and recorded my father's death date there. I also made a commitment to maintain that part of the bible, until that chapter of the family had passed. That was a difficult moment for me, but also a very important one, because it helped me appreciate how much richness I was experiencing from their things and from the process marking the end of their physical time with us.

When someone has passed away, it is true that they are physically gone. The scientific part of my mind knows that matter and energy cannot be destroyed but are interchangeable. The first time this crossed my mind was when my maternal grandmother passed away. I was totally at a loss for what I was feeling, and somehow, my scientific self stepped in to offer some sense.

Perhaps, all the love you mutually exchanged and invested while in that physical relationship transforms into energy. Perhaps, at a certain point, your grief process and things you've done to physically say goodbye complete that transformation. As a result, that physical absence converts into energy, a sacred love energy that allows all that remains to settle in quite nicely and safely into your heart, where they will always remain. Settling these physical possessions of theirs and sharing them with others aided both in my comfort and this transformation. I hoped that it helps for others, as well.

Neighborly Gifts

My dad was always interested in being a good neighbor and modeled this for those who knew him. It just came naturally to him. He was always telling me stories about different things that he did to help people out. There were a few first-time homeowners in the neighborhood over time, so he felt needed. I truly enjoyed hearing the other side of the story — the sides of the stories that he didn't know — from the neighbors' point of view. One of the stories that I loved the most was from a neighbor across the street. I had offered him my dad's ladders, as I was sure my dad would want to have some things stay in the neighborhood.

The neighbor said, "Oh, absolutely!" and then began sharing a story about a time when he was having trouble starting up a new lawn mower. There was an issue starting it up and he was trying to figure out how to start it when my dad came over, offering to help.

My father asked him, "What are you doing? What are you doing?" and made him back up and said, "You just hold the handle!"

Of course, here's my dad, eighty-something years old, pulling the crank and getting it all started.

When he told me the story later, he said, "Boy, he reduced me to feeling fourteen again, just like that!"

The neighbor also recounted stories about my dad's wintertime help; Dad would get up early and shovel people's walkways.

He said, "When it started happening in the morning, they were trying to figure out, 'Who the hell shoveled my sidewalk? It's only 6:30! Holy crap!"

So, he and another neighbor started this competitive thing: *Well, if he gets up at 6:00, we're going to get up at 5:30!* Soon enough, it wound up being that it wasn't even light enough to go out and shovel, but they were trying to get out there and shovel before he did. They weren't quite winning, but there was another time when they were very excited as they finally succeeded. It was when he came to visit me at Christmastime, and there were big snow storms; they shoveled and he had no say. He came home, found that they had shoveled his driveway, shoveled his walkway, cleaned off his car, and everything was perfect for him. They felt proud because they had finally really returned the favor and he couldn't do anything about it.

My dad was very good about giving, but he wasn't very good about receiving. I had many dialogues with him about the circle of gratitude, and how you need to be grateful when people do things for you. It's not just about giving, it's also about receiving graciously. This was good reinforcement of that.

CHAPTER FOUR

Personalizing the Medical Process

HELPING THE CAREGIVERS UNDERSTAND THEIR PATIENTS

When a person is admitted into a hospital, whether it's planned or by accident, there is much history behind the person and their body. It's important to try to create a level ground between the person receiving care and the medical professionals giving care. From my experiences, both as a patient myself and caring for my parents as they have been admitted, I can say that nurses are some of the most amazing, strong, giving, caring people. The more information that you can give them, the more they take it to heart and incorporate it into how they care for their patients.

Caregivers Can Be Such Gifts

The beginning of the end of my mom's life was with an accident. As much as I wanted to help, there was little that I knew about burns or what to expect. I found the nursing community in her burn unit to be incredible, not just with her, but also with us.

With her, they were cautious, careful, and attentive, but they also kept their eyes on us, calling to our consciousness our needs, saying, "The cafeteria's open now, perhaps you can go get a bite to eat. You can even bring something back here if you like."

They also coached us on the medical process, resources, and support networks. The more that we became open to the coaching—I'm speaking primarily about myself, here—I saw more coaching flowed. Their counsel included health issues that we were facing with my mother, but they also addressed our needs for support by suggesting counseling or ministered support and reading material that was available. Their support was exceptional and was freely offered from the time she was admitted through the day that she passed away. I valued this very much.

With my father, it was similar, but the outstanding support came mostly at the hospice center. They cared for and about him, and they cared about us as a family. The entire staff—nurses, doctor, chef, housekeeper, and minister—were open and available to talk. None of the care was rushed. It was very luxurious from that aspect. It allowed for a lot of interaction. Even at night, I received their support. I became afraid to regress to the family residence to sleep at night for fear that he would pass away without me there. As a result, they brought a fold-out chair to his room, so I could sleep there.

As they'd come in to turn him every two hours, to protect his body from bedsores, they would sometimes joke with me and say, "Do you want us to turn you, too? Are you ready to be flipped?"

There was such sweetness, care, and respect there. The more I let down my guard, the more caring I was able to receive. The nursing staff at the hospice was absolutely of the highest caliber.

The Impact of Elective Communication on Care

When my mother underwent her grafting surgeries, she was heavily sedated and essentially incommunicative. After the second surgery, all verbal communication ended due to intubation. I became more observant through our long hours in the burn center, and I noticed, as I mentioned in the previous chapter, that the nurses were speaking to her in a certain manner based upon assumptions gathered from our last name, *O'Boyle*. In actuality, Mom was first-generation Czechoslovakian and her maiden name was Pitel. I noticed they were calling her *Maggie* — a shortened version of her name, Magdalen. I recalled that Mom didn't really like being called Maggie very much; only my father called her Mag or Maggie. For everyone else, she preferred to be called Madge.

I found myself getting kind of irritated hearing some of these things, and thought *The thing I do have a choice over here is how I respond to what is happening.*

I pulled out my computer and typed a two-page note I've mentioned before, entitled, "Who is Magdalene Martha Pitel-O'Boyle?" It told her story and some challenges of her life. She was the last of six children from an immigrant family. Her father passed away when she was only nine months old, so she grew up without a father. She was the first person from her family who graduated high school. It told of her miscarriage and stillbirth. It shared short scenes of her life that evidenced how strong she was, what she had been through, and how she preferred to be addressed by the name Madge. Rather than asking them to read this, I taped a copy up on the wall, next to where they recorded her vitals.

A very fluid and inspired change happened. The first nurse who saw it didn't say anything, but over the next hour or so, I noticed different staff members coming in and making notes on the vitals sheet, silently reading what I had written. From that point forward, she was called "Madge" when they talked to her. It may have been me, but I felt a new sound and cadence in their communications with her.

Demands on staff are high in medical care facilities, though most medical staff still strive to do their best. Getting to know a bit more about patients may seem like a luxury, but I found it important to make my mom more tangible during a critical time in her life. As people age, it seems the earlier parts of their lives sometime fade into the background, and they may share less, brag less about their lives. I found that sharing a bit of my mom's life really did enrich the relationship and the caregiving style.

Being the Voice for Your Loved One

There were many times and reasons when I had to be the voice for my mom or dad.

These situations fell into three areas:

1. The patient is physically incapable of speaking.
2. The patient's personal behaviors or choices are misread.
3. The medical staff has a lack of understanding about the patient.

The first area is the most straightforward. This occurred when my parents were heavily sedated and could not speak, or when my mom was intubated. In these times, my voice was mainly to guide care or choices.

In the second area, misreading personal behaviors, I experienced this only with my father. There were two parts to this area: 1) outward appearance or behavior, and 2) personal choices.

In the case of appearance, there were two key examples that stood out. The first was when my dad was taken to the ER due to remarkable pain prior to his transfer. He hadn't shaved or had a chance to dress properly. I imagined his unkempt look led to some misconceptions about him, his means, and needs. He also chose not to use hearing aids, though he was quite hard of hearing. This led to many communication issues and assumptions on both his and his caregivers' part.

During his subsequent hospitalization, he also chose not to shave or be shaved for most of the two weeks, preferring to shave while standing up and looking in a mirror as a personal goal or milestone. As there are many people who come in contact with hospital patients, not all can know these goals, but many will be influenced by what they see with their eyes. I know this was true in my dad's case, as I observed such a change in the engagement of the staff when I finally convinced him to let me shave him. He was a good-looking guy with bright blue eyes, and he was quite friendly. The shave changed both the way he felt and the way he was seen.

Another two examples that fit into this category are regarding my dad's choices around pain management. His choices here were difficult for me to accept. The first was that he didn't want to be too much trouble and didn't want to bother the staff for help or pain medications. One of these incidences was when he needed to use the bathroom, decided to get himself up and use a bedside option unassisted. This ended in a very painful fall for him. He chose many times to forgo medication, even when offered, and rather offered his suffering up to God. In both of these cases, I tried to reason with him and intervene or coach the staff. I was largely unsuccessful here because of my dad's stubbornness and hospital regulations regarding patient rights.

The third area addresses a lack of understanding about the patient. I experienced this in both the hospital and rehabilitation facility with my father. When he arrived at the rehabilitation facility, it was just after the fall I mentioned earlier. He was in the hospital and he was in significant pain. My dad was both hesitant to trouble the staff to ask for pain medication and caught up in the cycle of offering his pain up to God. His pain interfered with his mood, mobility, and rehabilitation efforts. In meeting with the house doctor, we spoke and she agreed to try fentanyl patches to offer him relief.

In a previous chapter, I introduced how his physical and psychological reaction to the fentanyl was not noticed by the staff. It also led to his oxygen saturation dropping very low and his transfer back to the hospital.

Once at the hospital, the reaction appeared to be missed and only the oxygen saturation was being addressed. They interpreted his behavior as senility or confusion. When I learned of his transfer and made it to the hospital, I immediately saw the issue. He was experiencing a reaction to the fentanyl, as evidenced by a major irritation underneath the fentanyl patch, he was scratching his body, and his behavior was alarming. I demanded a pain specialist, the patch was removed, and his behavior normalized about a day and a half later. In both cases, his regular physician was not the primary caregiver because the rehabilitation facility had its own staff doctor, and the hospital had a hospitalist; they did not know him or his baseline and accordingly, were not able to manage his care.

Caregivers are in a difficult position. The demands and time pressures of their job are strong and perhaps increasing. Most workers in medical facilities are competent clinically, but there is more to care for than just the clinical aspect. This is where I tried to step in as an advocate by being there for my parents as much as possible, but I'd also take a walk down to the nursing station, call the doctor, and have conversations. There are times when your intervention may help slow the pace down and make space for quick and relevant dialogues that help to improve the care of your person through conscious, open-minded communication.

More difficult for me was to accept what I could not change, which was both the natural behaviors of my parents and their diagnoses.

DEALING WITH CHOICES

As I went through the experience of illness and loss of my mother and father, I realized, most times *after* the fact, that I was not as well-informed or that I was too rushed in making important decisions. These decisions did not make a difference in whether they lived or died, but rather a difference in how they, as well as we, felt about the type of care that they were getting. My goal here is to share some stories from which I learned a tremendous amount about making choices.

Know Your Resources, Research Your Choices

My father had been in the hospital for about two and a half weeks after his diagnosis with stage IV prostate cancer. As his hormone and radiation therapy were starting to take effect, it was now time to move him to a rehab center, where he would hopefully complete his treatments and then begin to regain his strength. The hope was that he would be able to return to and live in his home. The social worker with the hospital had offered me some alternatives of where to go, and I also had some discussions with my dad's physician about options. We knew this was coming, and I had a few days to decide. I took a tour of three separate facilities, drew conclusions based on what I saw and had read in reviews, but realized afterwards that I didn't consider all that I should have.

One of the facilities looked very nice and had some outdoor spaces to enjoy, but when I went there, I was a little concerned that he may not get enough care and attention. Another facility was smaller and a little bit more outdated, and I didn't feel that comfortable there, although the personnel were warm. The last place that I went to was newer, clean, crisp, and smelled nice. Reviews ranked it as a five-star facility, and I wound up choosing that one.

In the end, I was not satisfied with the facility for many reasons, but in addition to that, I did not realize that the social workers had kind of geared me toward places that would be covered fully by Medicare insurance. As a result, I hadn't included in my considerations

100 percent private facilities, or facilities that were less funded by Medicare, or even facilities that were a bit farther from the immediate area. I regretted not discovering and researching these, in particular after things started going south with my father at the rehab center.

I discussed my angst with my sister, and she was more pragmatic about this than I was. She had come to the conclusion that, "This is kind of the way that it is." She's in the medical field and has much more exposure to medical and care realities. I was still quite disheartened, which served as one of the drivers to my writing this book. I hope to convey my issues, and I believe there really *should* be some changes — ways to nurture the whole person and their families during these trying times.

There was a possibility that I had yet to come across with respect to my angst on this after my father had passed: *Maybe my father didn't want to get well. Maybe he didn't really want to communicate. Maybe my father didn't want to be relieved of his pain.*

While anguishing over my choices, was I distracting myself from these potential realities? Or was I turning my back on the reality that, no matter what I chose, he was going to pass away, whether it be in two months or two years? I felt like I was preparing for a marathon and not getting past mile two.

As time moved on after his passing, I gained a more balanced perspective. I became more forgiving of everyone along the way and, more importantly, forgiving of myself. It's the way it's meant to be. I found many of the things that pissed me off along the way were a bit of a distraction from the truth of my father's pending death; I just didn't want to let him go.

Choosing a Way Forward Despite the Odds

After my mother passed away, I revisited the choices we made, detailed in Chapter One, with mixed emotions. Did we take away her power of choice? Should I have pushed to discuss this with her, to include her in this decision?

We couldn't go back and change the past. I vividly recall that conversation and now know that, at that time, I was not present or strong enough to have that discussion. I also did not have prior life and death discussions with my mom that I could have fallen back on to help me. In hindsight, I knew that she was cared for extremely well during that time, that she was not in pain, and that perhaps it gave her soul, and ours, time to prepare for a separation. These thoughts allow me to come to peace with that decision.

Pain Management: Exploring Choices

My mom's pain was managed well, and she was monitored closely for signs of discomfort. My dad's pain was managed fairly well with Percocet in the hospital, where he was regularly prompted by the nursing staff to take something to address his pain. When he went to rehab, pain management fell apart. As he had fallen the day before his move, I knew he was in a lot of pain. When at the rehabilitation facility, he was reluctant to ask for pain medication. I did not know that, when in a rehab facility, the patient has to ask for pain medication. Additionally, they usually do not have opiates.

At a certain point, I realized that my father wasn't thriving there at all; he was declining in health, not eating well, and not able to participate in therapy. I believed it had to do with the level of his pain but suspected that the reality of his condition was weighing on him, too. I watched closely when they changed him or helped him get out of bed; he would cry out in pain, yet would not ask for pain medication. I requested a visit from the house doctor and asked if they had any other alternatives. As I've spoken about before, we went with fentanyl patches, a transdermal way to deliver some pain relief to him. That did help a bit, but I was unaware that there could be strong side effects or reactions, which he experienced.

I didn't think out of the box at the time; however, a year later, my daughter raised my awareness to several nonmedicinal alternatives she learned of while doing a paper on pain management in college.

Clinical studies have shown effectiveness of natural-based alternatives, such as:

- Massage
- Aromatherapy
- Acupuncture
- Meditation

Ironically, these were things that didn't arise in my consideration set in dealing with my dad, although I use these in my personal life. This is another area where I would like to raise higher awareness in hospitals and rehabilitation centers. Incorporation of these alternative therapies—in particular with people experiencing a high level of pain, like from cancer— offer additional ways to help manage the pain other than pharmaceuticals. They also have the added benefit of not interfering with awareness or digestion. In lieu of these alternative options being offered at a facility, perhaps it may be an option to advocate for them with your care team or to implement some of these yourself.

In our journey, a key point I tended to overlook was my dad's reluctance to either advocate for himself or take something when offered. Though I can only reflect back and guess why that was, I realize that my need to see him relieved of pain was not more important than how he wanted to manage his care. This was an area that we had not discussed during our many deep chats over dinner and wine, though I wish we had.

Choosing the Right Hospice

My dad emerged from the fentanyl reaction about two days after he was readmitted to the hospital. It was such a relief to see him back in his right mind and able to talk coherently with me. This relief was quickly erased by a conversation with his physician, who said he felt it was the end of the road, and it was time for hospice. Watching and hearing this news delivered to my dad, again in a very loud voice due to Dad's poor hearing, tore through me and left me weak. When the doctor left, I didn't even know what to say to my dad. I just held his hand, holding back tears; he seemed to resign himself to The News. I had thought this was just a crisis we could bounce back from but now was made aware that this reality was bouncing us out of the hospital and into hospice.

My dad had wanted to never leave his home until he died. I struggled with the fact that I understood this, yet knew we wouldn't be able to honor his desire for two reasons — the new carpet in his house, which wasn't yet finished, and the high level of 24/7 care he would need.

My sister and I were the only ones caring for Dad, and we both worked and lived quite a distance away from my father's home.

We needed to explore alternatives outside of his home. The frenzied search for an alternative led to some fast learning, but the personal cost of that was something I had to deal with later. As explained in detail earlier, although we knew our father would die, we hadn't thought to explore this ahead so, for us, I only had about a day to research and decide on the best hospice solution.

On top of the struggling to grasp the realization that the end was near, I then spent hours at that very pivotal time rushing around, trying to understand options, visiting facilities, and making that decision rather than being able to spend time with my dad while he, too, incorporated this news.

In addition to choosing the option that fits for you, there are also financial implications for each choice:

- Is the choice covered 100 percent by Medicare?
- Do you have personal resources to supplement the costs?

There were aspects of these questions that were not made apparent to me during my meeting with social services. As I reflected back on this time, I could have been proactive and researched this when he was in rehab, knowing that the end would eventually come. This would have required me to be really honest with myself and out of character with my optimistic nature.

The key thing that made me the saddest about not researching this ahead of time was time with my dad that I had counted on. After he got over his drug reaction, he was eating a bit again, he was actually conscious, and I could speak with him. But now, instead of being with him at that point, I was pushed into a flurry of activity rather than spending one or two days with him, when we could have just been together and spoken or sat in silence. I became most sad about this once he was moved to hospice.

Once he arrived there by ambulance, they needed to assess him and check him in. During the intake, they gave him IV morphine because they assessed his pain at a very high level. He was much more relaxed, so much so that he basically didn't speak from that point forward. I had now lost the ability to have those long, honest, tearful, loving conversations that I expected to have with him in hospice.

I was sad about that. *What was the last thing I remember him saying? Was there anything else I didn't give him the opportunity to tell me? Or tell my sister?* I longed for that last sound of his voice, similar to that last hug I had with my mom.

In my heart, I know that we don't miss out on things in life, reality unfolds exactly how it should, you are where you are, and life gives you the experiences you're meant to have. And, without this precise experience, I wouldn't have the ability to tell others in hopes of impacting the trajectory of their choices as they approach them. From this perspective, I am grateful, but there was a part of me that was truly sad about this for a long time. Sometimes the sadness would be overwhelming, and I would call his telephone just to hear his voice on his answering machine.

Nine months after my father passed away, my mother's older sister's health was declining. Her care team recommended that she be moved to hospice, and her family chose to move her back to her home for her transition. There were many family members around to be able to help with those last moments and her care. Her family generously gave of their time to be with her for that. It was a beautiful experience.

I can see how home hospice care can be great. Another friend, whose mom had a very sudden discovery of cancer with a very short period of time to live, chose home care. As she was still conscious for the first few days, it gave them time to look through pictures and talk about things for several days before she progressed to that point of needing high pain relief and dialogue ceased.

There's a space and a right situation for each of our loved ones' transitions. Though I often encourage being present to fully experience what is happening, I also see how honesty about the circumstances can require you to think ahead to create a plan before decisions suddenly come pressing in on you.

Physical death is inevitable.

My father used to say, "Birth is a fatal disease," and I had always thought that was a pessimistic way to look at it, but it is very realistic.

Being more conscious about the fact that life does end allows you to think about making choices that may make the process better and easier for you and your loved ones. It allows you to be more present during the process, if that's what you choose.

Until I was faced with my mom's death, I don't think that I ever thought about picking up a book and reading about this stuff, or thought much about it before it happened. I was much more involved in understanding the meaning of life and how to make my life rich and full. I see the dichotomy in my actions versus my recommendations. I felt compelled to write about this, so perhaps we will consider death as a part of life, rather than just the end of it.

THE IMPACT OF YOUR DECISIONS IN EACH PHASE

When you are faced with a crisis or a diagnosis that excludes an outcome of survival or recovery, you are confronted with something that can make you panic, become fearful, or scattered. Despite this, things still must be done to help the patient, to keep people moving forward in the hospital—things must still be done. The challenge lies in understanding what is normal protocol, when there is time to ask questions or when time is of the essence for decisions.

Questions help you understand what is expected or going to be happening next; they allow you to be better prepared, or slow everything down, so that you have a chance to incorporate decisions and the meanings of these decisions. Understanding when you do or do not have a bit more time to make a decision is important and not always clear. Following are some examples of when this was clear or blurred for me.

Ask Yourself, "What's Next and What Should I Expect?"

I shared some about moving my father to hospice. An interesting shift happened once we arrived: There was a profound change in the sense of urgency. The urgency and energy level that was felt at the hospital vanished. Hospice is about being there to die and, for this, there is no rush.

That was a little shocking for me. I began to enjoy the peacefulness of it, the reverence. But, that contrasted with my unmet expectations of beautiful slow, long, maybe cheerful or joyful discussions with my father. I envisioned he would have a little time to enjoy the beautiful view of the gardens, perhaps join me outside for a few last breaths of fresh air or streams of sunlight on his face. Instead, after his intake assessment, I found myself seeing that he wasn't speaking anymore, barely conscious.

I wondered: *When was the last time I heard his voice? What was the last thing he said to me?*

With my mom, I clearly remember the last time I heard her voice and what she said. Each night as I would leave the hospital, I whispered into my mother's ear about how grateful I was for the special bond that we had, that I loved her, and said goodnight. Though we always spoke to her, she didn't answer, but we knew she heard us. I clearly remember a day or two after her second surgery.

That night, after I had whispered that in her ear, she whispered back, "Goodnight. I love you, Anne."

That's probably the best thing you can ever imagine hearing as someone's last words— maybe that or, "I'll be okay."

It was such a gift that she spoke to me one last time. Had I understood what was next when we checked into the hospice with my dad, I might have asked for just a moment or two alone with him.

Know What's Covered, What Your Resources Are, and How It Impacts Your Choice

Financial resources come into play again when choosing a hospice setting. I've shared before that during the unexpected, short session I had with a social worker at the hospital, I had felt pressured a bit by the social work team to choose a hospice hospital for my dad. During that meeting, they focused a lot on what was and was not covered by Medicare. The explanation offered for this focus was the financial uncertainty you would face as the length of stay; in other words, how long it would take for him to die was unknown.

In general, they were saying, "You definitely want to have it covered by insurance, so that you're not running out of money, or it isn't going to cost you a whole lot. That's why you have insurance."

Although I was kind of hearing them and believing that, I afterward questioned myself and my sister as to whether it really mattered to us that much. Our father had some resources set aside, and we agreed that we were willing to apply them for the best care that we possibly could get for him. It was interesting that resources did not come up in that discussion with the social work team.

The facility we chose was not automatically, fully covered by Medicare and was subject to an 80/20 copay agreement. We later learned at the hospice that our dad's need for either constant oxygen or IV pain relief would make his stay eligible for 100 percent coverage by Medicare. His care team determined that this was the case for us, so his stay of fourteen days was completely covered, rendering any prior concerns or discussion about co-pays a moot point.

The key here is understanding what your resources are and what you are willing to commit. This information should be discussed with both social services, or whoever helps you select your care facility, and your care team. Allowing for an inclusive and open discussion while selecting a hospice setting will enable your teams to guide you in the best possible direction. The goal is to match resources and needs to select the best care possible. The same or similar principles would apply when selecting a rehabilitation or long-term care facility.

Navigating Communication with Family

Communicating difficult news to family is necessary but can also be challenging. In this area, we made some assumptions; perhaps other families do as well. In our family, *cancer* was a dreaded word that often was interpreted to mean someone was going to die. In my father's family, it was more prevalent than my mother's family.

A few years prior to my dad's diagnosis, his younger brother passed away from prostate cancer, so I was a little hesitant upfront to tell the family that Dad now had it, too. I knew that also telling them it was stage IV would be letting them know that he was likely to be passing away sooner rather than later. With my mother's accident, it was quite different; I'm not sure we were even fully incorporating what we were told, and the path was less straightforward. I was also worried about the impact The News would have on her sisters because they were in their eighties and nineties. We wanted them to know and pray for her but didn't want The News to cause more problems than we already had.

We organically gravitated toward working with a point person within each side of the family and relied on them to determine how much and how best to tell the other members of the family. This happened in both cases and worked very well for us. There were certain cousins we could be frank and open with, and this was helpful. My family also lived about three hours away from the ancestral home, so visits were not easy. In the case of my mom, she was in the ICU and visits would have been difficult at best. Both of my parents were also private, and this left us more to consider.

The family was supportive of the path we took. We were grateful for how much our cousins — Joe, my "bookend," and Edie, my "nurse" — supported us in this effort and carried the burden of conveying The News and updates to many of the family members. Limiting how often I needed to repeat what was going on was also helpful for me at the time. The more I talked about it, the more real it became for me. Most days were difficult enough with just the healthcare discussion and keeping up with my own family.

Afterward, I thought more about this and wondered if there wasn't more behind my need to limit my communication with family, friends, and colleagues. I discovered a thought cascade of mine. It went like this: the more that I repeated the updates, the more they became reality, as if I was speaking it into reality, in particular with the bad news. Speaking about it forced the gravity of the situation to the surface for me and forced my fears of loss to rise up.

Perhaps my use of point people also helped me avoid my fears. I held to my optimism and hope instead. I believed that my positive intention and prayers, and those of my family, would actually make a dramatic, positive impact on the outcome of my parents. Voicing out loud the updates — in particular, the unfavorable ones — was counter to the positive intentions I was holding and voicing daily.

When things weren't going well, I felt like *I* was failing — my intentions and prayers weren't enough. In verbalizing to people that my mom or dad was getting worse, it was emotionally hard. I felt like I was failing them, even though I knew that it wasn't my failure. My will to have them well was very strong and, perhaps at times, overrode the journey they had chosen.

Understanding and Managing Time Pressure

There were two times when I felt like I was being pressed to move more quickly than I felt comfortable. Both times, the need to make a decision was not medically urgent, and I was able to push back a bit. The first instance was when I moved my father to rehab, and the second was when we moved him to hospice.

Both times I needed to challenge the timelines presented in order to balance them against our needs. It seemed that, no matter what was happening with us, things just marched forward.

A key learning for me was first to understand the nature of a decision: is it urgent or not and why?

Speaking with the healthcare team helped a bit, but, in hindsight, I had not understood the nature of the urgency either times. Despite not knowing the nature of the urgency, I was able to slow things down. If confronted with this again, I now know to ask about schedules, insurance, medical outcomes, and rationale.

The second thing I learned was to make sure that I was listening, understanding, and asking questions, such as:

- What happens next?
- What can I expect when this is done?
- Are there other options that we have not discussed?

When you are not a medical professional, there is a frame of reference missing, and sometimes, you don't know what you don't know.

How can you get around that?

- Call yourself to be fully present.
- Ask questions.
- Take notes.

It is an emotional time and can be hard to focus. Review what you have been told and ask the questions again if you do not understand or come up with additional concerns. I found that healthcare professionals are amazing with information, but they're doing this every day; it is routine for them. It really is up to you to seek the clarity you need. I never felt intentionally misled or avoided. It was just a matter of taking the time and being willing to ask the question.

CHAPTER FIVE

There Are Many Gifts in a Loved One's Passing

RECONNECTING FAMILY MEMBERS AND FRIENDS

When someone close to you dies, it feels like there is a hole or a break in the circle of your loved ones. It is an opportunity to re-heal the circle of loved ones, as well. Though we were only following what we had seen our family do after deaths before, I found that the service and a meal together truly helped us reconnect with our family and friends on a deep level. I felt supported emotionally and imagined that the break in our family circle was reconnected. In my mind's eye, it appears like a large group, standing in a circle and holding hands. When one dies and leaves the circle, others step forward to join hands again and the circle is again complete. Once again, a source of love, strength, and support.

As we said our final goodbyes to our mom and dad, there were many touching things that happened and others that I wish had occurred to enrich that experience even more.

Healing the Family Circle: The Importance of a Service and a Meal

My mother and father had moved away from their family when my father got a job in New York, so we were at least a three-and-a-half-hour drive away from most of a very large nuclear family. When I was younger, we visited frequently, but as I got older, those visits became less frequent and centered more around weddings, funerals, and occasional holidays.

My family had a very traditional approach to deaths. There was a wake for a one-day period, a funeral the next day, and then a meal after the burial. There was ample opportunity for quality time with family to reconnect.

During the wakes and repass dinners for my parents, I enjoyed the stories that people would tell about my mom or dad, most of which I had not heard before. Whether it was told by family, friends, colleagues, or neighbors, it was a beautiful way to help each other through the grieving process and enrich memories on both sides of the story. At times, it was difficult and I'd find myself tearing up or crying. Almost always, there was someone to help me through that, maybe even helping me laugh.

My mother's funeral was very difficult on our children, and they were very disturbed seeing her in the casket. We were fortunate to have our relatives step in and help, many of whom were meeting the four children for the first time. A friend brought his dog along and helped distract them outside, playing with him in the parking lot. It was a beautiful release.

If you can be open to it, people really want to help you. These small and big expressions were such gifts to me.

We had a closed casket at my dad's wake and had many beautiful pictures of him in the room. During the family-only wake hours, an interesting thing happened with a beautiful outcome. I was sitting and talking to two of my mother's sisters who came. One was ninety-three at the time, the other was one hundred. I was sitting with them, and they were talking about their other sister, who was ninety-five. I had visited her when I was in Ohio. I was talking about posting pictures on Facebook of us doing a selfie.

The two aunts said, "What's a selfie?"

Immediately, I went to get my camera and started to show them what a selfie was. We got some really funny pictures upfront of them saying, "What's that?" Cute, funny pictures of our faces with the scrunched noses or smiles.

But then, a beautiful thing started to happen. Some of the kids recognized that we were taking a selfie, and they jumped in behind us. A beautiful series of pictures transpired as the whole family started joining in and photobombed us! It started off with me, my Aunt Annie, and Aunt Peg. Then the kids joined, next my sister, cousins, and aunts and uncles. In the end, we had everyone crowding in, standing on chairs behind us — twenty-five people just laughing, all captured in a picture by my brother-in-law's camera and mine.

Looking back at that, I'm sure it made my dad's heart sing. There's nothing better than having happy experiences at a wake. And, it is such a strong visual reminder that our family closed that circle around us that day. No longer could I feel that both of my parents had left me, and I was an orphan. I was completely surrounded and supported by my husband, my children, my sister, her children, my cousins, uncles, and aunts. I was surrounded by so much love, there was no way I could feel alone. I'm sure the funeral parlor thought we were nuts; my father would have liked that, too.

Funerals Are Reunions

My family is fairly far flung. Our parents lived a distance from their family and my sister and I many miles farther than that. It was similar for some of our cousins. As a result, our parents' funerals brought family from different areas of the country to support us during those times. It certainly is a sad occasion for the gathering, but it is a true gift how others show their respect for your parents or for you.

It is also an opportunity for many segments of your life to cross with family, friends, neighbors, colleagues, and more. I recall observing the room at different points, noting my dad talking to my boss, a colleague talking to my sister-in-law, and longtime friends reconnecting after a long time. If it were not for the wake, these segments of my life would not have crossed. How honored I felt that they were there. I felt raw, yet open. Some beautiful conversations happened with a new level of openness and candor. The exchanges that happened were genuine. Again, another gift.

Neighbors offered new perspectives on my parents through their stories, having seen more of them over the past ten years than I. A neighbor told me that one morning, looking at a mess in the snow, she wondered if my father might have fallen. As she looked a little bit more closely, she realized that my dad, at eighty-eight or eighty-nine years old, had thrown himself back in the snow and made a snow angel for her.

Another very pregnant neighbor locked herself out of the house, and my dad, in his early eighties, climbed in her window to unlock the door for her. My mom nurtured a neighbor back to health through meals, flowers, and conversation after the neighbor had breast cancer. A gift of a fancy umbrella and feather boa from my mom made quite a hit for a little girl's birthday. Cousins told me how much I reminded them of my mother when she was younger, what she looked like and about her energy.

There was incredible, genuine joy in these stories. They were priceless gifts shared in abundance. It drew me closer to many people. You see that there is much in common and much to gain from these interactions.

I found the whole process of a wake, funeral, and burial to be very spiritual, but also primal and grueling. I was spent. After all I had been through, along with the care I had not given myself, sitting down and having a meal with a group of loved ones seemed another way of satisfying a need to be nourished, both physically and spiritually. I had a deep need for my body to have nourishment, and my emotional body had that deep need to break bread with family and friends.

It was a smaller group and away from the venues I associated with sadness, so conversations were a bit more lighthearted.

A meal allows you to part from this loving circle in a positive way.

I remember as a kid looking back at the repass, saying, "Why are we doing this?"

I'm not sure that I really understood it until I was older and realized the importance of sharing a meal and being there for each other. Nourishing yourselves and nourishing your souls away from a sad venue is renewing. Although the reason for the reunion is sad, the gifts that flow offer hope and connection.

PEOPLE, STORIES, AND EXPERIENCES THAT TOUCHED MY HEART

People

Cousins

As my dad was passing away, I was staying mostly in touch with four people in the family: an uncle and cousin on my dad's side, and two of my cousins on my mom's side of the family. They helped a lot, because they took care of the details I gave them, then disseminated those to the family. I've mentioned that I didn't have everybody's cell phone numbers, I didn't have everybody's email addresses, and they had them all. Between these four people, I was able to talk to one or two, or email one or two, and then all that information went out to everybody I needed.

I think probably the most beautiful surprise for me was them telling me back, "Oh, yeah, thirty-five people are coming to the repass dinner."

I was almost stunned. We have a huge family, but that was a great number of people that actually were going to come three-and-a-half hours, maybe stay overnight, and then spend the whole next day with us. It was a gift that my cousins, with whom I had been really close while growing up, were still there — just like they were when I was younger, helping me every step of the way.

A Ray of Sunshine

I was lucky enough to meet my dear friend, Shaun, in New Jersey through an old boyfriend when I was eighteen. We have remained friends to this day. When I was going through the loss of my dad, it was great to know someone was nearby with whom I could blow off steam, have a glass of wine, or just accept her advice and hugs whenever I needed them.

After my father passed, she came over to the house to help me prepare for guests. The house was in disarray due to the flooring work, and many things needed to be put back into place. My father wasn't the best housekeeper, so we had a lot of straightening up and cleaning to do. She came over and was totally present to help me in any way that I needed. It was amazing! We brought out the cleaning supplies and declared all knickknacks, windows, surfaces, and corners free game while enjoying glasses of wine, sharing some amazing stories back and forth, crying, laughing, bitching, and moaning.

Her help and company were incredibly valuable to me. Over the course of a few days, we worked side by side. One time, she brought her daughter along to help out, and I was honored that she did that. Her daughter was sensitive, caring, and helpful; it seemed natural to have her there to help, and she reminded me of when I was young and quietly helped or observed the adults at times like this. I learned a lot during those times from my family. It felt we were carrying on a tradition from my childhood; this made me smile, and I'd like to think my mom was smiling, too. Shaun provided support that she gave without limits or constraints, and freely, thanking me the whole time for asking her to be a part of it.

I'm grateful, as I get older, for how profound relationships can be with people you may not spend that much time with anymore. I am lucky to have these golden threads of friends who weave themselves perfectly into my life. Perhaps the key to that is to simply allow your heart to always remain open and be grateful for these moments.

More Than a Helping Hand

Gary has been a friend to my husband, Dean, for ages. He has a flooring business and helped us out with the re-carpeting and flooring in our father's house. I don't believe he knew he was also signing up to be chief counselor, drink-pourer, and dinner partner for me, as well. While I was going through the hospice experience with my dad, Gary would be busy at the house and was usually still there when I returned home. He was also the first friend I encountered after I lost my dad and helped me through those very sad and difficult moments. I am still very grateful for that.

Gary had met my father only once at my mother's funeral, but through working at their house and seeing my parents' things, he got a sense of my father. He seemed to develop an understanding of him and, somehow, I think my father sensed that and was open to it, too. Gary talked to and consulted with my father throughout the day as he worked. I found that sweet and comforting.

I think my father felt welcome to try out some of his new skills after he moved to the Other Side. The day after my dad had passed, Gary was working on carpeting the stairs while we were talking about my dad. As he moved up a step, a picture, framed with wood and glass, jumped off the wall. It hit the steps, rolled down to the bottom of the stairs, the frame and the glass broke apart from each other and then the glass rolled into the kitchen, and then leaned itself against the microwave, without breaking.

The two of us looked at each other and said, "That's really interesting!"

That was the first of several *interesting* things that happened that, I believe, was my dad letting me know he was there and alright.

The next day, I needed to meet with the funeral director, and I had gone upstairs to change and get ready. Gary was still working on the stairs at that point. As he started to move up a step to progress with his work, another picture fell off the wall.

Gary said, "Whoa! Bill's talking to me again!"

"Well, of course he is!" I said.

"What do you think he's saying?"

"He's telling you, 'She's a married woman, get the hell downstairs while she changes!' "

We both had a good laugh.

In the days after my dad passed, Gary continued his pattern of playing music while he worked.

When I returned from the funeral home, he said, "I think your dad really appreciates music, but today we're sharing an inside joke, and I'm playing the Grateful Dead. Do you mind?"

"No," I said, "I think he's probably laughing, too."

Dean and I were grateful for the work Gary had done at the house for us, but his friendship was truly the gift.

Stories

A Picture Is Worth a Thousand Words

Bob and I also busied ourselves with putting together picture collages for the viewing at the funeral home. This involved enlarging two pictures of Dad that we would use in place of an open casket. One picture was of him in a jet with his bomber hat on as he prepared to fly; the other was of him on his eighty-fifth birthday at Fort Washington in New Jersey. There's a beautiful spot there that looks out over the George Washington Bridge and the Hudson River. I loved this picture of him; his blue eyes were bright and shining, and he looked happy and content.

The store that was enlarging and mounting these for us happened to be close to Fort Washington park, so I offered, "Would you like to take a little walk in the park where I used to go with my dad?"

Every year on my dad's birthday since my mom passed, I used to visit with my children, take everyone to the park, and walk around. It was a lovely spot amidst an urban area where we would see deer, chipmunks, and maybe hawks or a raven. My father had a love of nature, and it was a delight to share that with him like we did on walks when I was a child. Bob welcomed the idea.

We enjoyed the opportunity to enjoy a bit of nature together at the park and stretch our legs a little bit. When there, Bob and I decided to take a couple of selfies. I have two pictures of us by the bridge, at the same spot where Dad and I used to take our pictures. There is one of us smiling, and it just warms my heart because he looks and sounds like my dad. There is another where he spontaneously hugged me, kissing the side of my face. There is just such love shared between us in that picture in the same exact spot I shared that love with my dad. I love these photos because they feel like a celebration of family and offered a sense of completion to me. They are a gift that I'll always treasure.

Reconnecting the Family Circle . . . With Knots

I've spoken about my belief that funerals are a reunion; the healing of our family circle continued after most of the family left following my mom's repass dinner. Afterward, my father, sister, and I and our families went back to my parents' house. The stress of the past five weeks and funeral were wearing us out. My sister suggested that we get out and move, so we took the children for a walk at a small nature preserve in the area. It was a sweet spot, probably just a couple acres, in the middle of a suburban area that usually rewarded you with sightings of chipmunks, birds, frogs or turtles. It was good to get out.

While we were wandering through the paths, my son found some dried vine, and said, "Uncle Bill, put your hands behind your back."

He was really fond of his Uncle Bill and was enjoyed getting to know him better. Bill put his hands behind his back, and our son promptly tied his hands together quite well. His uncle hadn't known about the book of knots my dad gave our son; he had loved that book, studied it well, and practiced on anything often. He had become an expert at knots.

After a few tries, his uncle was unable to break free and said, "Okay, Chief, that's really cool! Let me go now."

"Oh, that's not why I tied it!" His response started some fun banter and laughter as we tried to untie him. It was a small, lighthearted moment I welcomed and seemed to make laughter okay.

A Lasting Remembrance

After my mom's funeral and burial, there were still many details that needed to be managed. One of these details was to create a headstone for the grave site. My father asked me to take the lead on this. The only direction he provided was that he wanted his name on there as well. I agreed and proceeded.

I attempted a design myself and sketched elements I felt captured interests or essences of my parents. The process was emotionally challenging; I wanted to honor them the best I could and, still reeling from the loss of my mother, was now also addressing the reality that my father would follow this path, too. I spoke with the cemetery caretaker and was referred to a wonderful small business that was willing to work with me to design the headstone, including the customized elements I had hoped to include.

We worked through several design iterations and settled on something that pleased us all. On my mother's side, I put a sculpted rose, representing her love of roses, and a sculpted a dove on my father's side, representing both his love of nature and the symbolism of peace and rebirth. A cross was centered on the stone and represented their love of the Catholic faith. Engraved into the cross were clovers, representing my father's Irish heritage and his love of clovers. No matter where he went, he seemed to be able to find four-leaf clovers on a regular basis. Several of the clovers on the cross were four-leafed.

Last, we included the words, *Always in Our Hearts.*

Coincidentally, the stone was engraved in Vermont, near where I lived, and provided another touchpoint between my parents and me. Even now, when I visit their grave, it gives me great peace that we created a beautiful space to mark their final resting place.

Through almost every part of this process, people rose up to walk me through what needed to be done during the process of losing, honoring, and remembering my parents. Through most of those steps, there were ways to customize and personalize every part of that process. This was of lasting comfort to me.

Experiences

A Visit From My Dad

My dad's youngest brother, Bob, was someone I have always felt close to, perhaps because he is the youngest of my dad's family. He shared family stories with me, he was open minded, and he was a patient listener. During my father's hospice process, he was one of the few people with whom I kept in touch closely. He offered to join me in the hospice, or afterwards, whenever the time was right. As the end drew near, we decided he would join me afterward. Two days after my dad passed, he arrived and we shared some time alone together.

Uncle Bob was a great help to me as I began planning the funeral. His strong knowledge of both the Bible and music were valuable to me in the planning process, and I was grateful for his knowledge and company.

One evening, while we were working on these details, we shared a unique and special experience. I had decided to take a break from the funeral planning to prepare for garbage pick up the next morning. The carpeting and flooring work left much to be disposed of for garbage collection the next day. As I headed outside to begin moving trash to the curb, I reached to turn on the porch light. Just as I turned it on, it looked like the bulb died.

I said, "Oh, damn, what a great time for the front porch light to go out!" Then, suddenly, the porch light flickered. Aloud, I said, "What?!" It flickered again, and I realized that it was clearly my father messaging me. I called Bob out to the porch and said, "Oh my God, you won't believe this. Bill's here!"

He said, "Excuse me?"

Just when he said that, the porch light flickered again, as if responding to his words.

I had become comfortable with what I believe was my dad's ability to connect with me through the earlier experiences with Gary and the pictures, but I knew this connecting was meant for more than just me.

I proceeded to say to Bob, "My dad knows that he can have access to me any time, but for you, this is probably a very special moment. I think I will take the trash out and leave you to talk to him for a little bit; maybe there are some things that you two want to have a conversation about."

I went outside, and I started moving things from the garage to the curb. The whole time I was bringing the trash out, this porch light was flickering on and off. This went on for a least a minute or two.

When I came back to the house, I said, "How did it go?"

Bob responded, "We were having a very lovely conversation, and I was telling him how he had very lovely daughters, and he should be very proud of them."

"So, does it feel complete?"

"Yeah."

I turned to the light and said, "Okay, Dad, thanks for coming and visiting again. That was really sweet!" The light flashed two more times, then it returned to a steady beam of light. I was pleased that someone else was there to experience that with me.

These times when my dad reached out to me prior to his funeral truly helped me understand that he was liberated from his body and his soul was soaring. It made the process of his funeral and burial easier on me and, even to this day, I still experience times when he and my mom connect with me in simple, profound ways.

Lighting a Candle for My Uncle and Hearing His Voice

The demands of my own family, home, and work left me less time than I would have liked to keep in touch with my extended family. I was honored to be drawn back into another uncle's life and able to close that circle with him as an adult before he passed away. Uncle Joe was my mom's brother. He was always my "Unc," the closest of all my uncles. I had a special bond with him. After he died, my mother passed along a life insurance check to me from my uncle, saying that it was for my children's college fund.

I thanked her, "Oh my gosh, I didn't know this was coming to me! This is wonderful!"

She said, "Well, show your gratitude and do something kind for him. Light a candle or something."

I chose to do just that and went to my local church with my children. We went in and lit a candle, and then I sat in a pew to pray for a while. When I started to say the *Lord's Prayer,* I heard his voice so loud and clear that I stopped praying and turned around to look behind me. I fully expected to see him because I heard his voice clearly. I saw only my children there, but I knew he was with us in spirit. That was the first time I knew he had that ability to be able to speak to me, and I had that ability to hear him.

The next time I heard his voice was three weeks before my mother's accident, when he alerted me that he was coming for my mom. In hindsight, I was relieved and very honored that I recognized and had this kind of connection with my uncle before he delivered The News about my mother. It was also very comforting to have him join me in prayer, hearing him praying along with me. It was beautiful.

Getting Woken by My Mother's Touch

A couple years after my mother passed, I was sleeping in my bed, and I felt someone touch me. I opened my eyes, expecting that it was one of our children. But when I opened my eyes, I saw a woman with longish hair, and a white, older-style nightgown, the kind my mother wore when I was growing up. It didn't really compute and, at first, I thought it was my daughter, that my eyes were deceiving me because I had just awoken.

I said, "Elaina?"

She looked at me and recognized that I could see her. I blinked my eyes one more time in disbelief but, when I opened them, she was gone. Although I only saw her for a second, I knew it was my mom. Though startled, I felt comforted by this. I'm not sure my husband shared the sentiment; I told him what had happened when he woke up. Though I found it amazing, I think it kind of freaked him out a little.

This visitation was validated in a meeting with my nieces a few years later. Somehow, we got talking about all these interesting spiritual things when we were out to dinner; they are open-minded young ladies and enjoyed hearing some of my stories mentioned here, though I had not mentioned my mother's visit.

One of them then said she had a story, too. "I remember when I was a little girl, and I would sometimes not sleep well at night. I would sit up in bed, and occasionally see a woman leaning over my sister, talking to her and whispering in her ear. She would turn around, look at me, and smile, and go back to whispering."

I responded, "Wow! Did that scare you? How did you feel about that?"

She said, "No, no, she was just talking to her. It was nothing. It was fine."

I kind of got a funny look on my face, and asked, "What was she wearing?"

My niece got a bit anxious, and said, "Oh no, why are you saying that? What do you know? What do you know?"

I said, "No, no. Just tell me what she looked like."

She literally described the same vision that I had seen. At that moment, I realized that it really was my mother who visited. What was unusual was that my niece's visions happened while my mother was still alive. I knew my mom wanted to be a grandmother so much, and having her grandkids far away from her was difficult. If I were trying to explain this, perhaps my mom was traveling in her sleep by spirit and visiting the girls while she was alive. Perhaps it was her way of still being present for them. We all had a beautiful, teary moment, reflecting on how much love she showered on us all.

A year or two later, my other niece called me and let me know that she too saw the woman in the white nightgown turning a corner in her house. She now had gotten a glimpse of her herself. It was quite an experience to share. There is much more that is possible when we allow ourselves to be open to experiences. Perhaps our energy or spirits, after passing, are only a dimension away. Maybe we don't have access to them, but they are still very close by.

CONNECTING WITH THEIR SPIRITS

The journey of understanding my own spirituality and negotiating my relationship with the death of a loved one started when I was nineteen, when my grandmother passed away. I remember leaving her repass dinner with my father and him driving me back to college. During our ride, I recall seeing beautiful beams of light streaming out of the clouds and down to earth. I remembered somewhere in my mind that someone once had said that this was God reaching down to take the soul back to Heaven. It seemed perfect that I was seeing this on the day of her funeral. It started my mind thinking. My grandmother was a strong, kind person and the matriarch of my mother's family.

I thought: *What happens with all of that? Her energy, her love, her strength. Where did it all go?*

My scientific mind stepped forward. I recalled the law of conservation of mass, "Energy cannot be created or destroyed, it can only change form."

I revisited that law, along with many other thoughts, over the next few months, and spent much time talking about this with my college roommate. I also began reading and reaching for answers, and one of the first books that I reached out to was *Out on a Limb,* by Shirley MacLaine. I remember a section where she talked about a former partner who had passed away. She had finally stopped, became still, on a mountaintop, and then she felt him come to her. She could actually hear him speaking, and had a dialogue with him.

I remember thinking: *Holy crap, that's really cool! I hope that happens to me!*

I guess that wish from when I was twenty came true. As I and my family got older and beloved relatives passed away, I opened my heart more and more to the possibility that death was not the end. My avid pursuit of myself, my own beliefs, and my true nature led me to a space where I was open and thought it possible that I might have some of these phenomenal experiences. The next few stories are about some of these amazing experiences I have had, where I have been comforted by loved ones' souls after they have passed.

Spiritual Retreat Becomes Spiritual Reunion

I meditate daily and I avidly read and work with thought leaders remotely and in person as part of my commitment to learn more about myself and my spirituality. One particular encounter led to a greater connection with the spirits of my parents. In exploring my life's direction with a coach about six months after I lost my dad, I questioned where I'm meant to go in my life, what I'm meant to do. We spoke about my work but also about my experiences through the loss of my parents. Though I felt drawn by the desire to write about this, I hesitated, even though encouraged by this coach. About six months after that, I attended a three-day spiritual retreat and, of course, this book was on my mind.

At the retreat, I experienced a transference of Divine energy or love. During this transference, I felt able to connect deeply with this love and had the most beautiful experience. As I relaxed into the energy or love, I was ushered by angels to a space of beautiful light. The light was brilliant though not blinding and there, I felt great peace, stillness, and love.

As I looked around, I saw my parents standing in this light. There they were! Both of them were waving their hands in front of them, like they were cheering me on, and I listened to them say, "Go! Go! Go! Do it! Do it! Do it! You've got to do it!"

I was stunned.

"Really? You're okay with this?" I asked with my mind.

They responded immediately, "Oh my gosh, we're good with it! Go!" It was amazing, because I knew that they were giving me their approval to write the book. When this vision ended, tears of joy were streaming down my face. First, because I was able to hear *and see* my parents together in this joyful way, and second, because the one thing that I had angst over, they resolved for me by giving me their blessing. Though this would be the first time I visited with my parents in this manner, I am grateful it was not the last.

I always had two hesitations about this book. The first one was the deeply personal nature of these stories; I was cautious about sharing them because they reveal some of my personal beliefs and nature. The second hesitation encompassed the very profound and deeply personal experiences that I had with my parents. I had a deep sense of honor and privacy about these losses and did not want to defy their confidence, reveal too much, or violate their memories by sharing this publicly. My parents were private people, and they kept a lot to themselves. I was grateful for this experience at my retreat, because it was the green light for me and resolved the internal conflict that I had felt. This green light was reinforced several times during my writing process.

The next, and the last, green light was to talk with my sister, tell her some of these stories, and ensure she too was alright with my sharing. I was surprised at myself, that I hadn't shared some of these stories with her before that time. It was a relief to be able to do that with the only other person I had known all my life. Two weeks later, I found my publisher at my local farmers' market and so, the stories are now shared.

I am grateful for the journey that began with the death of my grandmother and how it began a more dramatic opening of my heart. Life continues to unfold in amazing ways. I am much more at peace with myself, the profound experiences I have had, and, of course, the connections made that leave me with a sense of gratitude and love.

Conclusion

Most of all, I want to leave you with a feeling of hope! Death can appear to be devastating, final. Perhaps these stories, my musings, and the epiphanies that I have had will crack open the door for you to see that death is a process. It's not an end. It's another phase of life, which gives back more as you embrace it. The key to unlocking these gifts is to truly be present, as much as you possibly can. The more present you are, the more aware you will be of the gifts that come from someone's passing.

My ultimate hope is that this book can be read in advance of losing someone, or maybe even during the process of losing someone, so that you can have the richest and best experience possible. If it moves you, pass this book on to someone else after you've read it. Perhaps it will start conversations that need to be had or journeys that are waiting to start.

I am very grateful to be able to share my journey, my thoughts, and my process with you. And, I am grateful for the people in my life — past, present, and future — who have helped me grow, learn, and experience a very full life, a life to die for.

Next Steps

You can connect with Anne, and follow her work at the following places:

Website: ToDieForbook.com, for helpful links and resources

Blog: ToDieForbook.com/blog, to sign up for her newsletter

Facebook page: ToDieForbook

YouTube: https://www.youtube.com/channel/UCR0pACVuJde1YNzthtfISQA

Instagram: To.Die.For.book

About the Author

Death was never an event Anne's parents sheltered her from as she grew up. They took her to a wake for the first time at the age of two. Though only one of two children, Anne is from a large family with an abundance of opportunities to see that many struggled with loss for many reasons. When Anne finally lost Baba, her maternal grandmother, it was the beginning of her journey to develop a personal understanding of death, spirituality, and life's meaning. This event, when she was twenty and starting her junior year in college, started deep conversations with her friends, intensive reading, classes, and sessions with several spiritual teachers and intuitives.

As Anne explored, she was also aware that her intuition and inner guidance grew, as well. The first time she connected with someone who had passed was in 1992 at the age of thirty, following the death of Evelyn Isadore. Though not with great frequency, she has, since then, been visited by close relatives upon and after their passing.

She learned that anything from action to acceptance to stillness can allow you to see the gifts that only a loved one's departure can bring. She welcomes you to explore what gifts you too may find in that loss.

Anne was born in Pennsylvania and raised in New Jersey by her parents, along with her sister. She attended the University of Delaware and Hunter College, receiving a BS and MS in Nutrition, which led to a thirty-year career in sales, marketing, and business development in the food industry.

Anne is grateful for the time, travel, and resources her career has provided that allow her to continue her quest for growth.

She now resides in Vermont with her husband, their two children, and their dog, Moose. She enjoys the amazing communities in Vermont and all things local. She is still inspired today by her mother's love of gardening and cooking and her father's curiosity and love of nature.

Ten percent of all profits directly and indirectly related to this book will be dedicated to hospices and improving access to hospice care.

"A spontaneous family selfie at our father's wake
still brings me joy today."